James Plunkett was born in Dublin in 1920 and educated at Synge Street Christian Brothers School and at the Municipal School of Music. His collection of short stories, *The Trusting and the Maimed,* was published in 1959 to wide critical acclaim. It was followed by *Strumpet City* in 1969 which was an international bestseller, subsequently adapted as a television series and sold to fifty-two countries. A book about Ireland, *The Gems She Wore,* was published in 1972. His stage play, *The Risen People,* was written for the Abbey Theatre and first performed there in 1958. It has been revived regularly since. On its appearance in 1977, his novel *Farewell Companions* became an immediate bestseller. In that year, his collected stories were published by Poolbeg Press.

James Plunkett has had a long career in radio and television and has written and produced plays and features for both.

HEALY

James Plunkett

The Boy on the Back Wall
■■■■■■■■■■■■■■■■■■■■■■■■■■■■■■
& Other Essays

POOLBEG

A Paperback Original
First published in 1987 by
Poolbeg Press Ltd,
Knocksedan House,
Swords, Co. Dublin, Ireland

© James Plunkett 1987

ISBN 905169 60 3

Cover illlustration by Helen Pomphrey
Set in 11 on 12 Baskerville by
Busby Typesetting of Exeter
Printed by The Guernsey Press Co Ltd,
Vale, Guernsey, Channel Islands

Contents

Acknowledgements

Poolbeg Press wishes to acknowledge the following publishers and broadcasters for material appearing in this book:

Hibernia: for 'Orpheus, His Lute'; 'Salud'.
The Irish Independent: for 'Away to the Hills'; 'Keep the Home Fires Burning'; 'Mother of Seven'; 'Remembrance of Things Past'.
The Irish Press: for 'It's No Go, My Honey Love'.
The Irish Times: for 'The Inferior Appetites'; 'O Child of Misfortune!'.
Open Door: for 'Beware of the Dog'.
RTE Guide: for 'Rambles in the Past'.
The Sunday Tribune: for 'I Hear You Calling Me'.
Tara Mines Limited: for 'Dear Harp of My Country'; 'The Minstrel Boy'; 'The Offering of Swans'; 'That Solitary Man'.
Telefís Scoile, RTE: for 'On Being Ourselves'; 'On the Nature of Poetry'; 'The Parting Guest'; 'William Wordsworth'.
Thomas Davis Lectures, RTE: for 'Changed Times'; 'From Hero to Artist'; 'The Mission of Discontent'; 'O'Casey and the Trade Unions'.

Preface

The essays in the following pages are a few of the many written over the years in response to the requirements of occasion or to satisfy an editorial whim. Some, for instance, are biographical sketches marking such events as the centenaries of national celebrities who, although they teeter perpetually on the verge of disappearance into oblivion, have the strange knack of floating as shadowy, under-the-surface presences in the collective Irish consciousness. The potted biographies were aimed simply at restoring what had been entirely forgotten about them, or at filling up the gaps in what was yet remembered.

Others are concerned with aspects of literature, originating in that extraordinary temptation to scribble which has afflicted so many of our fellow countrymen, from the successes or failures of the few who won mastery to the many who ultimately despaired.

There are four talks for young people about poetry and its nature. These were commissioned for Radio Telefís Eireann by Maev Conway Piskorski with the request that they should aim at engaging the imagination and sympathies of the students as a supplement to the more academic insights which were being adequately supplied.

For the most part, however, the essays concern themselves with personal experience and observation of the felicities and contradictions of the world I was destined to grow up in and the general characteristics of its sons and daughters: elders who had been shaped by the effects of a national uprising, a marathon trade union upheaval, a civil war and the founding of an independent state – all these sandwiched between two world wars.

Perhaps what follows will add its own little say-so to the numerous other efforts to reach an understanding of our general gait-of-going.

James Plunkett, July 1987

For Frank O'Connor,
the boy who once sat on the back wall,
in grateful memory
of his interest and encouragement
and his many kindnesses

1

O Child of Misfortune!

Then child of misfortune come hither,
I'll weep with thee tear for tear
THOMAS MOORE

It was a black, rain-sodden morning on the first day of the working week and as the bus listed dangerously rounding the Bank of Ireland corner it threw up a shower of muddy water that drenched the three of us who were standing on the open platform. The elderly man beside me got it in the face and on his shirt but when he had wiped it away he resumed his almost absentminded survey of the saturated streets before making his comment. When he did so he was resigned, unresentful, impassive.

'Typical oul Mondah,' he said.

The three of us, being Dublinmen, agreed. We had been reared in the same conviction. The worst is inevitable and must be endured.

That was in the late thirties when your Dublinman studied a serene pessimism which, to give him his due, seldom let him down. He believed that opportunism, nepotism, corruption and crookedness were observable phenomena rampant in everything except his own immediate and entirely unprivileged circle. The Dublinman hadn't an earthly. One of them summarised it for me once when he explained that while a countryman would get away with stealing the horse, a Dublinman would be hanged simply for looking over the stable door.

There was much to justify his philosophy of total rejection. In the pre-Treaty city his overlords had despised him for being poor and distrusted him because he was, after all, Irish. The post-Treaty State, which his phlegmatic brand of heroism had done much to create, began its career with an all-out drive to reduce his wages. Having dealt with that through his old stand-by, *The Union*, he was faced with the charge that he was not, after all, Irish enough. He was instructed to become more patriotic by venerating thatched cottages, Gaelic football, traditional music and the Irish tongue, all of them equally incapable of plucking at his heart strings. As the Dublinman saw it, the new order, determined, as per usual, to destroy him, had mustered an invasion of professional Nationalists with peculiar accents and remote rural roots who were planted in highly paid jobs in order to denigrate and undermine his indigenous legacy. They deplored his passion for cross-channel football coupons and English Sunday newspapers, his interest in Dixie Dean and Liverpool United or Arsenal or Sheffield Wednesday. Soccer football, he was told, was a garrison game. If he danced an old-time waltz, which was about all he and the missus could manage anyway, it was a betrayal of the National heritage. If he had fought in the Boer War or the Great War, as was quite on the cards, it was a matter for scorn and even shame. The final insult was to hear Tom Moore, that decent Dublinman from Aungier Street whose immortal melodies were the centrepiece of every Sunday evening singsong, described as a shoneen, the latest word (by all accounts) for a lickspittle.

He took the onslaught with a practised and implacable disinterest and listened to the enthusiasts not for what they said, but to seize the earliest opportunity for changing the subject. Their general behaviour bore out what he had often suspected: that he was the only man of sanity and good sense left in the world. And when they had gone he characterised them for anyone with a shred of interest:

'A tá-sé-fought-bled-and-died class of a merchant,' he

decided. Or, in the words of another with a more literary cast of mind who was describing a similar encounter to me:

'There was this tweed clad gael,' he explained, 'festooned with fainnes.'

Not that the Dublinman was unpatriotic. At the highest he had been flogged on a barrack square for being a Fenian or had fought with Pearse and Connolly; at the least he wept often enough into his pint while someone obliged with a few bars about the Boul' Robert Emmet, the darlin' of Erin. But he was inclined equally to reminiscences of his experiences at the Dardanelles, and joined with emotion in the chorus of 'Pack up Your Troubles' or 'Keep the Home Fires Burning'. The truth was that his culture was devious and even contradictory. It worked because of his innate toleration and realism and because he had enough good sense (as I have remarked somewhere else) to know that culture is a totality in which contradictions are harmonised.

To grow up in such a world, where the classroom in its turn was attuned exclusively to the ultra-Gaelic legacy, could be confusing, but only temporarily. You adopted the inherited armour which was invulnerable to fashionable ideological enthusiasms and returned to the cradle of measurable truth, located in the kitchen on weekdays and in the parlour on Sundays or whenever there were special visitors.

For me, as often as not, this was my grandmother's house near the sea. The parlour, like most in Dublin, had never finally acknowledged that the age of Victoria had crossed the bar. There were the usual ageing geraniums waiting to catch pneumonia from a breath of fresh air. There was a china cabinet displaying the family pieces, all far too precious to be actually used. In one of the pictures on the wall a young man descended the balustraded steps of an enormous mansion to a waiting carriage while his stricken parents clasped each other and looked on. In case the playing cards scattered generously about the scene were not enough, the title 'The Gambler' had been supplied in ornate script underneath. The gramophone cabinet in the corner offered John McCormack

and Franck's 'Panis Angelicus' or, if the mood were deter-
minedly intellectual, a selection of Fritz Kreisler's concert and
salon pieces. In the midst of all this, on certain afternoons,
my grandmother and mother were to be found closeted and
gossiping over illicit pinches of snuff. I was privy to the
proceedings because fetching it was a weekly commission. (At
this interval, I feel free to reveal all). The journey took me
to a little shop known as Snuffy Byrnes, where besides snuff
and clay pipes and twist tobacco there were bundles of
firewood, piled up coalblocks, a drum of paraffin with a tap
that dripped occasionally into assorted measures, fizz bags
which sometimes contained a whistle and lucky drumsticks
through which you could now and then lick your way to a
concealed farthing or even a halfpenny.

Nothing in that city was discarded that could possibly be
re-used. The Rag and Bone man visited regularly to re-
circulate the debris, offering coloured balloons or marbles or
spinning tops from his crowded barrow in return for jamjars
and old rags. On Saturdays we sometimes searched the bins
and the laneways ourselves to make up the money for the
pictures, rooting for empty Baby Powers for which the publicans
would pay us a few pence. Chemists and dispensaries expected
you to bring back the bottles. A suit of clothes could have
several lives because of the brisk market in secondhand goods.
Poorer children saved their boots for the winter months. If
they had none to save they went barefooted unless charity
intervened. Large sections of the community lived their lives
in the cast-offs of their betters.

Nevertheless, there were natural compensations. The
Phoenix Park belonged to everyone, from the shawled women
hawking apples and oranges to the gentlemen of privilege who
played polo. Sandymount and Merrion Strands offered bathing
and picnics to hordes of poor families, as well as the opportunity to pick cockles for stewing when times got worse
than usual. The mountains were easily accessible by way of
country lanes where in autumn blackberrying added to the
pleasures and profit of the journey. It occurs to me now, as

I look back, that there was never any need to lock your bicycle.

When did it begin to change: those tottering backlanes loud with vigour and community, the elegant streets where tall houses stood firmly by good manners and dignity? And how did they slip from us so quietly: the man who played the concert harp at Merrion Square; the other with the barrel organ and his little monkey who hopped down with his bag to beg your charity; the milkman who filled your jug from a tin measure and always added a tilley for the cat; those shell-shocked ex-soldiers re-enacting old battles along cobbled streets? Soon it was no longer possible to crowd an opentopped tram on the way to Shelbourne Park or Dalymount, or to travel from Harcourt Street on the train past Carrickmines and the viaduct soaring over the glen of Leighlinstown. Even the walk by the Shellybanks to the Black Lighthouse was destroyed.

A man once remarked to me that if they managed to shift Nelson's Pillar so handy, they'd shift anything. Another, impassive, detached, a mere passer-by as it were, said the whole bloody place was falling down anyway. They were both Dublin men. Louis MacNeice, who wasn't, nevertheless hit off their inherited, unchanging and unfailing philosophy:

> The glass is falling hour by hour, the glass will
>   fall forever
> But if you break the bloody glass, you won't hold
>   up the weather.

Now you're talking, says the Dublinman. He knows the future looks even worse. Typical oul Mondah.

(1973)

Orpheus, His Lute

When I think back to childhood and my first brushes with the mysteries of music I recall in an extraordinary way the smell of rosin. It pervaded everything. Then I think of a large window with sunlight falling through it, a music stand with a book of studies on it, and the torture of stretching the little finger of the left hand until its pitch corresponded to that of the open string next to it. It seemed a bit senseless at the time – all that agony for a sound that could be got without acrobatic fuss by simply bowing on the open string. It was an alternative I wanted passionately to put forward but I never summoned up the necessary spunk. The fiddle, I remember, kept sliding from under my chin. I used to worry about that too. Was the fiddle too small or was my chin inadequate? Or my neck too long?

Practice was another ordeal, especially if it had to be done in the front room near the road. It always gathered the neighbourhood kids. They made faces through the window, whined in chorus and sawed away at imaginary instruments. Learning music was regarded as a slavish surrender to adult notions of culture and respectability and this was a legitimate demonstration of their contempt. It was worse having to carry a fiddle case through the streets. Everything stopped, even fist fights. Irish wit and humour became the main dish on the menu. 'Ey, Jem – play your banjo', I don't know how many times that was flung at me. I realise now that the kids who yelled it were so underprivileged they regarded Synge Street as a snob school, but at that stage I had no social conscience whatever and would have brained them if I could.

I suppose it was inevitable that I should go to music. It ran in the family; not spectacularly, with child prodigies who performed before Queen Victoria at the age of seven or infants turning out fugues, but humbly as befitted our station in life. The grandfather made his own fiddles and played them after a fashion; my father had a medal which proved he had performed on the fife in a band which won a competition in 1911. Various aunts played the piano and one, for a while anyway, actually taught it. She supplied the heavy stuff at the Sunday night musical gatherings, in between 'O Breathe Not his Name', 'Yes, We have no Bananas' (sung by the uncle who had always been, well . . .a bit wild) and 'The Moon Hath'. I don't remember what the pieces were, but I recollect that when she sat down everybody said shush and the father would push his bottle of stout well out of arm's reach and become very solemn and cultured looking. The pieces were very long. She could cross her hands.

Later I did some professional playing on my own. My first fee was sixpence and a bunch of grapes. I was looking into a fruiterer's shop on my way from a lesson when the woman invited me in to play something. I could hardly draw the bow across the strings but she was easily pleased and rewarded me handsomely. My second fee was about half a crown, picked up one Saturday morning (I hadn't practised and was dodging a lesson at the time) during an aimless walk along the South Quays. Some foreign sailors called me on board their ship and prevailed on me to go through my repertoire. This consisted of short pieces with titles like 'The Gollywog's Dance', 'On the Swing', 'Stately Minuet' – pallid enough fare for seagoing men, God knows, as I well realised. However, I knew 'St Patrick's Day' and 'Father O'Flynn' by ear, much to the delight of the sailors, who clapped their hands and shouted 'Whoo' and then sent round the hat. I found myself leaning to the opinion that European audiences were more discerning.

Perhaps it was then the thought occurred to me that there might be a career in music.

There was, in a way. I graduated as most musicians did in those days, playing first with amateur music societies and providing chat music at high class dinners, then for opera and ballet and eventually with the Radio Eireann Symphony Orchestra, where my professional career ended. After a few seasons I came to the conclusion that as a professional I was a bit of a fraud. I felt I wasn't good enough and got out.

I'm glad I did. I had been playing chamber music with love and devotion since the age of sixteen or thereabouts. Once professionalism was ruled out it became the only ensemble playing worthwhile. Jem could play his banjo to his heart's content, at leisure and in intimate good company, with always enough in the bottles to mellow the performances. After countless sessions of the chamber music of the immortals music becomes an indistinguishable part of the personality. Like memories. A sheet of music, a stand and sunlight through the window, a glass of stout, the scroll of a fiddle and the resinous dust about the bridge are not merely symbols of gracious living or agreeable sounds, but represent an additional dimension to creation.

(1974)

Rambles in the Past

When I first started to work for a living there were colleagues – the elderly ones of twenty-two and twenty-three – who liked the Continent, for reasons that ranged from the scholarly to the sinful. These were the avant-garde, authorities on new novels and foreign affairs, conscious intellectually of being a cut above buttermilk. Most others preferred the Isle of Man, or the Channel Islands, or their pale shadows at home. The general idea was a beach, a funfair, slot machines, late night dances, a hotel slightly better than they could afford, drink, and picking up women. The war started before I had any occasion to make my choice, so I settled for holidays at home, mainly on that mainstay of Dublin life in the 40's – the bicycle – in an Ireland stripped suddenly of its signposts and mechanical conveyances.

I have never regretted it. There were no cars, no tourists. Only empty roads, flanked with trees, hedges, gates and fields. Sometimes they crossed rivers by way of graceful, venerable bridges, with occasional trains to be seen at the distance of a field or two, propelled by wood, turf, apple peel, potato skins – and sometimes even by railing posts ripped in fury and despair from the nearby fences. These were the quietest days ever in the forever quiet places of rural Ireland. Nothing happened, nothing whatever.

I do not mean there were no people. One day I spent two hours listening to a man in Barnes Gap who knew the prophecies of Colmcille and saw a straightforward connection between the present war and the Black Pig. Another time I played music with a man in some lost cottage in Donegal; he on a homemade melodeon, I on a fiddle he had put together out of an orange-box. And there were always neighbours in the pubs of an evening to tell you the weather was unlikely to change, or that Hitler was getting a cut above himself. A Wexford woman of incredible age who had sailed in the coffin ships pointed out a stake sticking up from the ebbed strand, and told me how a landlord had once tied an unfortunate tenant to it so that the incoming tide drowned him. 'There's good bastards and there's bad bastards,' she told me, 'but that was a bad one.' Very true. There is a hierarchy among scoundrels; they have their seraphim and cherubim, their thrones, dominations, principalities, powers.

Later I went to Paris, a beautiful city, reaching it after a twenty-four hour journey, when the lights along the Rivoli and the Champs Elysées made the night sky above them look like a calm, green sea. But there were no mountains. This absence of mountains eventually nearly drove me mad. I thought I was going to be very literary in Paris, but found that I was only lonely. There was so much of that formal beauty which so delights some, and so depressed Synge. It depresses me too. The pleasure garden exalts snugness and despises nature. The more ornamental the pond, the less is it like a lake. The world is neither snug nor wholly flat and should be seen not to be. Mountains are a Sign. Without them there is nothing very much to believe in.

Since then I have been to a few places: to Stockholm, a middle-class city where the night signs are beautiful above the waters of the harbour; to Riga where, looked at from a high window at night, the black-coated figures trudging in the snow under dismal street lighting look like a scene from the silent cinema; to Moscow, with fur-clad shoppers eating ice-cream; and many other places, including Tiflis, with its unshaven policemen, who smoked on duty, and its numberless public statues, every one of them turning out on close inspection to be Rostovelli, the national poet. He was, I am sure, a fine poet and the amiable Georgians are right to be so proud of him. As the Parisians are right about the first city of Europe and the Londoners are about Westminster Bridge and the Mother of Parliaments.

For me, all these were too large, and yet not large enough. I had been spoiled by the hey-day of the bicycle. I liked to be able to look through a familiar gateway to a familiar field, and from the field to the mountain, and from the mountain to the sky. I still do. There must be a river, with a pool to swim in and room to fish in. Enough to drink in the evening, but not so much as to take the edge off the following day. There should also be time for a little work. Work that is near the heart is always agreeable. So, at least, have I found it. So, too, though the bicycle had yet to come, did the Irish monk, labouring over his smooth lined book in the peace of the sunlit woodland, some twelve hundred years ago:

> In a green cloak of bushy boughs
> The cuckoo pipes his melodies
> Be good to me God, on Judgment Day!
> How well I write beneath the trees!

(1978)

Away to the Hills

In my formative years and those of my father's generation there existed among native-born Dubliners an unshakable belief that to desert the cobbles and the tramcars in favour of a life in the country was the sign of a basehearted traitor or the unfortunate consequence of a general softening of the brain. I remember being warned against the hazards of country existence by no less a person than Brendan Behan himself. I told him I had rented a cottage in Glencree with the idea of spending weekends in it and he was appalled. 'Would you not be afraid,' he warned me 'of being bitten by a mad sheep?'

It seemed the like had almost happened only a few weeks before to a friend of his who had been foolhardy enough to venture out beyond Dundrum.

The ban on country visits was not quite total. Picnics to the Scalp and Enniskerry were pleasant and good for the children. Hikes to Pine Forest or the Hellfire Club or Kilmashogue were health-giving. There were some damn fine pubs along the route of the steam tram from Terenure to Blessington. And from all these you could and did return the same evening.

My own loyalty to the generally held attitude was undermined in my early years by my parents and aunts and uncles. They tended to go into the country quite regularly and to bring me with them: excursions to Glendalough; train trips to Bray or Arklow; or just blackberrying to Fox and Geese at a time when I was so young that, although the name charms me even still, I cannot for the life of me remember where it was. Then they went further and began to spend whole weeks in farmhouses and hired cottages among the fields and the mountains and the unease which was to afflict me ever afterwards took root.

It was not that I had rejected the life of the city or the companionship of my fellows. We still rambled the streets and rode on the backs of bread vans when the opportunity offered. We wandered the quays and learned the names and nationalities of the ships as they came and went. We went to the pictures for the Saturday or Sunday matinee and to football in Shelbourne or Dalymount Park. There were Army Tattoos during Civic Weeks in the RDS where in the floodlit grounds we cheered as Sarsfield and his horsemen blew up the siege train at Ballyneety or Fitzgerald and his brave troops desperately defended the bridge of Athlone. There was an unforgettable week when a band of Cossacks came to Lansdowne Road and their display of reckless horsemanship included a scene in which a huge bonfire was lit and the riders faced their horses towards it and one by one jumped through the flames. We later lit a fire of driftwood on Sandymount Strand and with bloodcurdling yells did the same thing on our imaginary steeds. There was seldom any shortage of homemade excitement.

Nevertheless the heart was beginning to pine for what lay beyond. Stand on the iron bridge spanning the river basin at Boland's Mill and the mountains beyond the railway stared you back. Walk on the breakwater near the Half Moon Swimming Club and they surrounded you. Turn the corner of a street and, as like as not, there they were again, peering over the rooftops and the squat gasometers. I began to wish I could get out to them.

So I joined the boy scouts. The boy scouts were a disputed area. Some of our crowd held that keeping your shoes polished and doing at least one good deed a day were both disgusting and contemptible. Others, like myself, were prepared to stomach all that because we liked the idea of carrying a bowie knife on our belts and found the hats remarkably like those worn by the Mounties. There followed hikes to the mountains and eventually camps at weekends and for a whole fortnight during the summer. Certain simple accompaniments to the routine of camping filled me with delight and still do: the odours of tent canvas and the rubber smell of ground sheets; the feel of dew in the morning on bare feet or through canvas shoes; river water and soap and the tingle of sunburn; woodsmoke curling and its faint odour in the air. Early one morning in Glencree I crept out of the tent while the rest were still asleep. The valley lay wide and empty, there was birdsong and the scent of hay, the white crown of mist on Kippure was adazzle with sunlight and sent weblike ribbons trailing down its slopes. The world was drunk with its own beauty.

For a while it triggered off a poetry writing bout, not in imitation of the respected contributors to Palgrave's *Golden Treasury* favoured by the Establishment, but more like the trail-busting swagger of Robert Service.

> I have tramped the dusty highways
> I have tramped the lanes and byways
> In the crisp of clear Spring mornings
> In the mist of Summer dawnings
> Through the Autumn's gentle glowing
> Through the Winter's cheerless snowing
> I have heard the lonely calling
> Of the moorlands, falling, falling
> From grey-veiled hills I've watched the sunsets pale . . .

And so on. The echoes of the Old Sourdough himself are not hard to detect:

> I am the land that listens, I am the land that broods
> Steeped in eternal beauty, crystalline waters and woods.

Later on, the Youth Hostel Association took over where the boy scouts left off. An Oige had a network of hostels throughout the country with a choice at the beginning of the 1940s of nearly seventy routes between them for walkers and cyclists in the Dublin/Wicklow area alone. The overnight charge of one shilling for seniors and sixpence for juniors (under twenty years) covered the use of bed and blankets, together with cooking utensils and fuel. I remember two highly enjoyable cycling tours using hostels and affiliated hotels: one in 1938 to Trá na Rossan hostel in Co. Donegal by Newry and Omagh and Letterkenny; another in 1942 by Limerick and Killarney through Glengarriff and Cork and back by Cashel. The army was on massive manoeuvres at the time and one came across columns of men slogging along remote roadways or resting in groups on grassy ditches.

But it was hostelling in Wicklow that fed the desire to live in the country – to be precise, in mountain country – until it became fixed. One trekked by mountain and valley between Baltyboys (near Blessington) and Ballinclea (Donard) and climbed high up over Glenmalure and across into Glendalough; by the vale of Clara and the military road, over Kirikee mountain and on to Avoca. Rathdrum and Wicklow were within walking range then and from there it was back to Glendalough and on next to Knockree Hostel. The last leg was almost always from Enniskerry village to Dublin.

Hopes for a country cottage materialised at last in 1950. Marriage and children had severely restricted the weekend wandering, so we were happy to come upon a small but habitable one in Glencree valley under the shadow of Mount Maulin. The rent was nominal. It was sheltered by the sloping ground and had a mountain stream tumbling on its course a few yards from the front door. There was no electricity and no laid-on water, and, of course, no means of cooking except the open fire, which served well enough however, when supplemented by a primus stove. Water could be fetched from the stream which gave an unfailing supply. For lighting we acquired an assortment of paraffin lamps which included a couple of Aladdin lamps that worked on paraffin but gave light by means of a gas-type mantle, a Colman Quiklite in which the kerosene had to be pumped and pressurised (it had the bad habit from time to time of getting blocked up and threatening to explode) and ordinary paraffin lamps that operated on only oil and wicks. An Elsan in a rough shed around the back looked after the natural necessities.

Back in the 1950s the Glencree river had a reasonable supply of brown trout plus a leavening of rainbow trout which, I believe, came down from the stock that had been introduced into Lough Tay at the head of the glen by the Powerscourt family. Nowadays, with the increase in the number of cars and the greater accessibility of the roads, the river is pretty well fished out.

The people of the valley included a fair number of the descendants of the yeomanry who came over originally to Powerscourt Estate and a smattering of families with Ulster names. These were descendants of troops from O'Neill's army who took refuge in the outer wildernesses of the glen during the long and hazardous retreat after their defeat at Kinsale in 1601.

At least two poets had lived in the valley at one time or another. One was J.M. Synge, who had wandered extensively over Wicklow searching for solitude and an idiom and setting for his work. He stayed occasionally in McGuirk's cottage near Lough Bray at the head of the glen – the visitors' book held his signature and that of Frank Fay. He also stayed there in the summer of 1907 for some weeks while Molly Allgood (Maire O'Neill), the young Abbey actress with whom he was in love, stayed in a cottage down the road.

The other poet was Joseph Campbell who lived a hermit-like life in a cottage on the floor of the valley near the banks of the river, with its fairy rath and huge glacial boulders and the few remaining trees of what had been a primeval oak forest. He had been involved in politics for a period and was interned in the Curragh during the Civil War. Disillusionment caused him to turn his back on the world for much of the time, feeding his imagination on folk beliefs and the ancient sagas. Of Glencree he wrote:

> This grey earth is holy,
> From the sun-stones of Mashog
> To the seven eyes of the rainbow
> In the still water of Tea.

As a younger man he had written the English words to songs collected in remote areas of Donegal by the composer Herbert Hughes. The best known of these were 'The Ninepenny Fidil', 'The Spanish Lady' and that exquisite air, 'My Lagan Love'.

After the rebellion of 1798 a regiment of Highland fencibles was directed to cut a road across the mountains from the village of Rathfarnham to Aghavannagh, linking up the military barracks of Glencree, Laragh, Glenmalure and Aghavannagh. The one in Glencree later became a reformatory and later still a refugee home for children from Europe after the Second World War. The officer in command there during the aftermath of 1798 was Major General Sir John Moore, whose death at Corunna was recorded in a poem by Charles Wolfe:

> We buried him darkly at dead of night
> The sods with our bayonets turning;
> By the struggling moonbeam's misty light
> And the lantern dimly burning.

Also in the glen was Crone House, which had its own historic associations. Lady Wilde used to spend the summer there when Oscar and Willie were children.

So there was plenty of interest and plenty for the children to do: swimming in the river in summer and having picnics on its banks; fishing, gathering loose wood from the forest to start the fires with; exploring on the mountain slopes and along the forest paths. They made friends with the neighbours' farm animals – notably with a pet pig which answered to the name of Marty and trotted everywhere after them, just as a dog would. It became increasingly hard to pack up after the weekends and head back towards the city. It became more so when the city itself began in little ways to change its character and lose familiar things which had been part of its charm.

But there was no question of commuting. Children had to be able to get to school and bread and butter had to be earned. In addition there was much fetching and carrying to be done which, although it could be coped with for weekends and other short periods, might not be so manageable on an ongoing basis.

It was 1970 before a real possibility of making the move arose.

The children had almost finished schooling and there was a cottage in the area which we were able to buy. It had electricity, which was an advantage. But to make it habitable water would have to be brought in, sanitation laid on and cooking facilities provided. We also needed more physical space than its original size could offer. A water diviner found a water source for us and we brought it to the surface after drilling down 113 feet through solid Wicklow granite to get at it. A builder began work on adapting the original structure to our requirements and adding on what was necessary for our needs. It was ready for permanent occupation by September of 1971.

Needless to say, there were snags. One problem was getting professional help when things went wrong, as they did – with the water pump, for instance, and the central heating. We found we had no real contacts in these matters because in the city they hadn't arisen and in our previous country living they simply did not exist. On one occasion clothes which had been lying for some time on a bedroom floor were found to be warm. The reason was eventually discovered: water that had leaked in from outside and filled up the space under the floor boards was being heated by the central heating pipes that passed underneath the floorboards. But in time we established contacts with reliable service agents who see that the inconvenience of breakdowns is kept to a minimum.

Electricity power cuts, especially during storms, are more frequent than they would be in the city so we use gas cylinders for cooking, but there is nothing we can do about the lights and, worse still, nothing we can do about water. When the pump stops, the supply for domestic needs and washing and lavatory facilities just closes down. If this happens when we are snowed-in (usually for a few days about twice a year) then we are in real trouble, but it is at times like that that the essential kindliness and thoughtfulness of neighbours comes to the rescue and tides us over until a solution is found.

At first the last two schoolgoers used small motor bikes for the journey to the city, which was all right in summer but less than satisfactory in winter. There were spills on snow and ice, torn clothes and bruises and, a couple of times, barely avoided injury from following traffic. The solution was to acquire an old banger and draw up a solemn covenant about absolute equality in each other's use of it. At least it had four wheels and kept out the weather.

The younger people in these areas – that is, the young mothers – can be kept too much on the go ferrying the children to and from school, to and from music lessons and other extra-curricular activities and come to feel that instead of living in the country they are living in a motorcar. It is a situation which drives some of them back into the city.

For us, however, that no longer arises. The children are now all independent. My own journeys into town are few and when I get there I often wonder why I bother: most of the old landmarks have disappeared, the pollution is appalling and there are great gaps in once familiar streetscapes. It is not the city of my memories and affections and, if advancing years make it impractical to stay where I am, it is not to Dublin I would wish to return. The years have swallowed up the old city. I don't like what they have put in its place.

(1985)

Beware of the Dog

In my schooldays, I remember, travel to the ordinary individual meant simply trips down the country or, at most, safaris to places like Liverpool or the Isle of Man. Locations on the continent – never mind further afield – were places of exotic ambition to be attained only by the very rich or by those whose livelihood it was to sail the seas. The most an ordinary being could hope to do was to pore over the school atlas and dream up phantom journeys or wander down to the Port of Dublin to gaze at the cargo ships and catch in the unfamiliar languages of the crews some vicarious glimpses of faraway places. Or so it seemed to me as a schoolboy until, in the year 1934, the unbelievable happened.

A Holy Year was declared and the Boy Scouts, of which I was a member, decided to charter a boat to take about 1,500 of us on a pilgrimage to Rome. The all-in fare was only £10 a head (the civilian passengers helped to subsidise the scheme), and we arranged to save up the required amount over twelve months.

So, one fine day in March of 1934, instead of wandering along the river wall watching the ships sailing off to foreign places, I myself stood aboard ship and saw all the familiar landmarks gliding past me as quietly as if in a dream.

The ship was the SS *Lancastria* and we were destined to see – in addition to Rome – a little bit of Spain, a little bit of Gibraltar, the town of Ceuta in North Africa with its Foreign Legion (Spanish) barracks, Naples, and near Naples the part of the journey I was to remember most vividly: Pompeii, the ancient town dominated by the volcanic Mount Vesuvius.

One morning in AD 79 that volcano, after behaving itself impeccably for centuries, suddenly burst into frenzied activity, catching the people of Pompeii unawares. For three days it poured tons of cinders and ashes and pumice stone on the city. Day was turned into night, thousands of people were trapped by pouring lava while others only escaped by dropping everything they were doing and fleeing away. The volcanic ash buried the city completely, so completely indeed that in time people almost forgot it had ever been there. It was all of 1,700 years later when the historians set about digging it out again bit by bit.

And that's how it came about that my friends and I were able to walk its streets nearly 2000 years after it had been destroyed. For one romantic-minded young boy the experience was unforgettable. We walked the streets and looked at the walls of its houses; we even saw the charred remains of the nuts and fruits and loaves of bread that the people had left behind when they fled to escape the lava and the terrible rain of fire. We walked by the wine shops and examined the sentry boxes used by the guards; we saw the deep ruts worn in the paved stone of the roadways by the traffic of chariot wheels. And, to bring it all up to date, on a flagstone outside the gate of one of the houses were carved the words:

CAVE CANEM

We had enough schoolboy Latin to be able to translate this:

BEWARE OF THE DOG

There were grim remains too: a soldier stretched in death at his post whom the ash had coated thickly and transformed into a stone statue; a dog also, to which the same thing had happened. It lay with its legs bunched up and its neck twisted to one side in a last agony.

That visit awed me as much in memory as it did in actuality and inspired a schoolboy poem – a sonnet, no less:

I walked in old Pompeii when the sun
Dipped westward and bent to bid adieu
Saw old Vesuvius raise himself to view
The mute remaining of an age undone
Still line on shattered line the houses run
A silenced theatre tier on tier where drew
Poets the dreams they wrought, the tale anew
(Shadows by erstwhile shadows shadow spun)
And all was still. Along the dusty ways
No spectre moved, no stirring of the grass
Rimming each creviced flag, no legions march;
A sundial sits to stare the passing days
And no one notes. The swift years pass
And Time broods silent in a broken arch.

As verse it has its shortcomings; but it triggers off the excitement and awe of that walk down the streets of history even today.

The *Lancastria,* a wonderland of a ship which we all fell in love with as young boys will, became a troop carrier in the war and was torpedoed, and now lies somewhere near the Bay of Biscay. Every now and then, even still, at an age when life should have slaughtered the last ounce of romanticism, I think of her deep down there in the darkness and silence at the bottom of the sea, with barnacles gathering on her and ghostly seaweed covering a table I once sat at and a bunk that, as a boy of 14, I once dreamed in.

(1985)

Keep the Home Fires Burning

I remember when I was a very small boy, standing at a window with an elderly relative and looking out at a brown and threatening sky and a street which had grown suddenly quiet.

It was that hush which descends just before snow begins to fall. It must have been about this time of year too, because I remarked with excitement how wonderful it would be if we had snow for Christmas.

To my surprise, the idea was greeted with shocked disapproval. I was told I was a heartless little wretch with no thought at all for the poor, barefooted children who would suffer as a consequence.

I thought the rebuff unfair. I still do. As children the association of snow and Christmas had been hammered into us. Every Christmas card, every Christmas supplement of the daily newspapers, every Bumper Christmas number of the popular magazines was emphatic on this subject of the essential snowiness of Christmas.

Snow surrounded every Christmas crib I had ever visited, snow inevitably reflected the star that shone above the kneeling shepherds. It was impossible to visualise the Three Wise Men without seeing the powdery puffs of snow rising step by step behind the hooves of their camels.

Snow at Christmas, like the rainbow after rain, was a kind of covenant. I had had a sudden vision of snow which was like that in the carol of Good King Wenceslaus: so holy, so magical, so incomparably deep and crisp and even. Yet when I mentioned my vision to a devout and kindly old lady she immediately thought of slush.

Snow completely monopolised the Christmas greeting cards of childhood. I list, with affection, all that repetitious paraphernalia: The robin redbreast on a bough in the snow; the yuletide log being dragged home through the snow; the holly leaves bowed down under the weight of snow; the candle in the window spilling its golden light out on to the snow; the coachman and his coach all buried deep in a blanket of snow.

One idle afternoon, looking at the array of robins and candles and coachmen on the cards on the mantelpiece above the leaping fire, I passed the time by celebrating them all in Christmas card verses:

> These holly leaves and berries red
> As hopefully and brightly glow
> As any leaves or berries did
> On greeting cards of long ago
>
> This robin redbreast on a bough
> Is blest with immortality
> And many a verse and card will grace
> For generations after me
> By snowbound roads this coach and four
> And coachman muffled to the ears
> With all his jolly company
> Travel unaging through the years
>
> Then take once more the candle tall
> And set it shining through the gloom
> The mazy ways, the rutted roads
> For all their hazards lead to Home.

Looking at the Christmas cards of today, these motifs seem to be losing their time-honoured place, mostly to high quality reproductions of appropriate scenes from the art galleries of the world. But the snow, I note, still holds its own.

The slow, pre-Christmas days of childhood seem in retrospect to have been spent hugging one's knees in front of the fire under the cards on the mantelpiece and the coloured streamers reaching from the centre of the ceiling to the four corners of the room and listening to the wind moaning to itself in the chimney, with smells of cooking perpetually haunting the air.

Either that or kneeling on a chair with that other great filler-inner of the idle hour – the photograph album – open beneath the double-wick lamp on the centre table. In it reposed a world which had run its course and gone on its shadowy way ages and ages before. It had great-grandfathers with heavy moustaches and stiff collars and massive watch-chains and great-grand-aunts with tiny waists and enormous hats. More absorbing still, it was choc-a-bloc with pictures of young men in uniform and newspaper clippings of things that had happened in the First World War.

The album had its quota of Christmas cards also, sent from France to the loved ones at home and these too were reminders of a story of the war which one of the clippings had recorded.

It told that on Christmas Eve 1915 the sentries on the firing steps in the freezing trenches of the Somme noticed that a strange and unusual quiet had settled over the barbed wire and shattered debris of the battlefield. Then, as they listened with ears pricked and eyes alert for any threatening movement, they heard from the opposing lines the faint sound of German voices raised in song and made out the words: 'Stille Nacht, Heilige Nacht.'

When the carol came to an end, the Germans called out over the intervening distance: 'Merry Christmas, Tommy'. And the sentries answered: 'Merry Christmas, Fritz.'

Then they stuck their hats on the ends of their rifles and raised them above the parapet. A little later, heads began to appear.

Eventually men from both sides climbed bodily over the parapets and Allies and Germans mingled in the middle of No Man's Land, exchanging food and cigarettes, shaking hands and singing carols together.

Then, when goodwill and fellowship had had their adequate

say, both sides returned to the blood and dirt in the trenches behind the barbed wire and in the morning returned to the duty of being enemies.

When word of it got abroad there was horror in high quarters and orders were issued that nothing of the kind must ever happen again.

Retelling that story to us and reading aloud from the biography of Father Willie Doyle, the heroic wartime Army chaplain, were favourite pastimes of my mother when bedtime approached and the housework had been laid aside. Most of the cards in the album were from my father in France to her at home. They got married when he returned in 1918.

My mother was a woman who loved Christmas and all its trappings and trimmings. We were dragged in and out of shops in search of suitable presents. We had to trail after her while she searched Moore Street from top to bottom for the Christmas ham and the turkey (and sometimes a goose) and hang around while she bargained and cajoled and jibed and pretended outrage at the price being asked.

All her life she was a compulsive and relentless bargainer. But she (and my father too) believed in pantomimes for children and in all the preliminaries: the coffee and cakes in Bewleys; the box of chocolates; the lemonade and biscuits during the intervals.

On Christmas Day she had a small Christmas tree on the table, a rare thing at that time when Christmas trees had not become customary in Ireland.

It was artificial, of course, about 18 inches in height, festooned with tiny candles which broke her heart by dribbling their multi-coloured juices on our best tablecloth. But when the time came for my father to pour whiskey over the plum pudding and set it alight she would have recovered sufficiently to enjoy the proceedings as heartily as we did.

It was also her custom, in the days after Christmas, to lead us on a conducted tour of the Christmas cribs of the city to decide which was the best. My memory is that the Oblate Fathers of Inchicore nearly always came out on top.

The Bumper numbers of the popular comics and magazines which came out for Christmas kept us occupied too. Those for children had simple crosswords and rhymes and games to play and puzzles to be answered.

Q. Why did the kitchen sink?
A. Because it saw the door step
(frenzied hilarity).

The more sophisticated ones combined a polite literary tone with the nostalgic and the seasonable. Samuel Pepys, for some reason or other, nearly always merited an airing. Perhaps because of his love of life and his tendency to see it with forthright clarity.

'*April 5, 1663 (Lord's Day)*. To church, where a simple, bawling young Scot preached.

'*Dec. 27, 1663* . . . So after dinner to the French church, but come too late, and so back to our own church where I slept all the sermon, the Scot preaching, and so home'.

The favourite, however, was Dickens. *A Christmas Carol* popped up in abbreviated versions and found its way into school concerts as a stage adaptation. Ebenezer Scrooges and poor Bob Cratchets abounded, while Tiny Tims responded to a multitude of toasts with the never-changing ever-repeated formula: 'God bless us, every one!'
Pickwickians at Christmas time were predictability itself:

Up flew the bright sparks in myriads as the logs were stirred. The deep red blaze sent forth a rich glow, that penetrated into the farthest corner of the room, and cast its cheerful tint on every face.

'Come' said Wardle 'a song – a Christmas song! I'll give you one, in default of a better.'

'Bravo!' said Mr Pickwick.

'Fill up' cried Wardle. 'It will be two good hours before you see the bottom of the bowl through the deep rich colour of the wassail; fill up all round, and now for the song'.

Thus saying, the merry old gentleman, in a good, round, sturdy voice commenced without more ado:

My song I troll out for Christmas stout
The hearty, the true and the bold
A bumper I drain and with might and main
Give three cheers for this Christmas old
We'll usher him in with a merry din
That shall gladden his joyous heart
And we'll keep him up while there's bite or sup
And in fellowship good we'll part.

The song was tumultuously applauded – for friends and dependents especially were in perfect ecstasies of rapture. Again was the fire replenished and again went the wassail round . . .

So went by the Christmases of childhood and youth. The season always brought a boom for cinema and stage – even in the forties, when wartime fuel shortages forced public transport off the roads around 9.30 in the evening and shows as a consequence had to start as early as seven in the evening. Nevertheless, they managed.

In the Radio Eireann offices in Henry Street there was one particular window which looked down on Moore Street and framed the whole bazaar-like scene that became ever more congested as the days led up to Christmas, a hectic turmoil of shopping bags and parcels and milling bodies which compelled one to stop and look down in delight.

Fruit and vegetables were piled on barrows that stretched the whole length of the street on either side. Paper chains in a multitude of colours and Christmas decorations of every shape and size cluttered the stalls. Tinsel gleamed and artificial frost glittered. Children's toys and packets of starlights and contraptions from drums to tambourines designed to make every conceivable variety of noise were being hawked on the pavements and in the middle of the roadway. The voices of the dealers rose up above that window like the steady pounding of a storm maddened sea.

Needless to say, because of the season that was in it, we took our turn to go down among the busy throng and take a seasonable glass or two in our favourite haunts – The Tower Bar or Gerry's, 'Little' Madigans in Moore Street and 'Big' Madigans in Earl Street.

Needless also to say, in the company of the best entertainers the country could supply, indiscretion was not always avoided. One colleague on his way to work on the morning after one such evening was menaced by a large, unfriendly dog which blocked his way and bared its teeth at him. He thought of the state of his head and pleaded with the animal. 'Bite,' he begged, 'but for God's sake don't bark.'

Has Christmas changed? Of course Christmas has changed. The Jimmy O'Deas, the Joe Linnanes, the Paddy Crosbies – and so many others – 'all gone', as T. S. Eliot put it: 'Into the dark, the interstellar spaces.' We ourselves must necessarily change, since we live in a world which changes so around us.

At the beginning of Advent, in the church I attend on Sundays, there was a change too. Or rather – a going back. By the Altar stood the Jesse Tree, and in front of the altar there was the Advent wreath. The tree is a symbol of Christ, with the six-pointed star of Israel on the bottom and the Cross as its blossom of fulfilment on the top. The wreath symbolises the coming of Christmas and it has four candles, one for each week, which are lighted in turn as the four weeks go by, to represent the coming of the Light into the world.

Both tree and wreath date back long beyond the robin redbreast and the coachman muffled to the chin – away back to medieval times, when there were little plays performed and dances danced about the altar, because all that was enacted in the worship was seemly and acceptable.

There is a story that a poor acrobat from a medieval circus was called to Christ's service and accepted as a servant by the Abbot of a monastery. He was unlettered and slow of wit and quite unable to learn the Latin or even the simplest of the routines of the monastic discipline.

It was also discovered that he left his cell during the night on mysterious errands which puzzled and caused the Abbot anxiety until one night he heard strange sounds coming from the chapel and crept down to investigate.

There he found the acrobat turning cartwheels in front of the statue of the Virgin and the Child. Then, the cartwheels exhausted, the acrobat took balls from the pocket of his habit and began to juggle with them. These were his only talents, and he offered them to Christ in his simplicity.

In a year or two, perhaps the tree and the wreath will have company.

(1985)

Remembrance of Things Past

Forty is the old age of youth (Victor Hugo once remarked) fifty, the youth of old age. He omitted, so far as I know, to say anything about sixty-five. Whether I like it or not, I am now qualified to examine the matter at first hand.

The main symptom of being sixty-five seems to be a compulsion to look back over all that space of living on the chance of finding some sort of purpose in what went on. Yeats, addressing himself to the same problem, sifted meticulously through his experience of childhood and youth in an effort, as he put it, to bring the balloon into the shed, by which he meant that he wished, before he shuffled off this mortal coil, to possess the whole of himself, a not uncommon desire.

It is surprising how far back those memories can reach. There is one of mine with a habit of returning time and time again for the past sixty-three years. In it I am a child – not yet two – lying halfway between waking and sleeping in the spare bed in the semi-darkness of my grandparents' bedroom in Irishtown, then *County* Dublin. Downstairs they have finished supper: I can hear remotely the sound of crockery being cleared. These are quite usual bedtime preliminaries, soothing and reassuring, and I have drifted almost totally into sleep when the sound of motor engines and a sudden volley of shots jerks me rudely into wakefulness again. My screams bring my aunt and my grandparents pounding up the stairs. They calm me and then my aunt stays with me until the terror dies away and sleep takes over once more. There had been a Black and Tan ambush a street or two away and I learned of that when I was a few years older. I have been puzzled ever since to know how a wordless infant could sense so unerringly the menace that lurked in the sounds of that night.

The bedroom itself is an ineradicable memory too. It overlooked the public road and when cars passed at night (very few in those days) their headlamps struck into the darkness and swivelled from wall to wall like a lighthouse beam and disappeared again in an instant. On a small altar in the room stood a statue of the Sacred Heart with a tiny red-globed lamp that cast a yellow circle of light on the ceiling immediately above it. My grandmother, who was a religious soul, was also superstitious. If the little lamp was allowed to go out through some oversight or other she went about predicting inescapable visitations of heavenly disapproval.

It was in that bedroom too that, as my four- or five-year-old mind grappled, as it quite often did, with a knowledge of the uncertainty of one's lifespan and the apparently inescapable certitude of demise, I stumbled on the fact that if I lived to be eighty I would have reached the year 2000 and straddled the breadth of two millenia. The ambition to do so took root and persisted throughout childhood.

I remember that grown-ups in the 1920s still talked about the Great War and the Easter Rising of 1916, about the Troubles and the Civil War. Memories of incidents during curfews, searches and raids and of violent deaths were still fresh enough to be fireside topics. In my own family the albums now contained photographs of young men in khaki (some of whom had been killed) and Remembrance Day divided the city into two camps : one the mourners with poppies in their coats; the other the protesters who wore lilies. Snatching the poppies was a pastime for the would-be patriots.

In 1924 Jim Larkin's return from the States and a long sojourn in Sing-Sing reawakened adult memories of that other epic event – the lock-out of 1913 and its partisan tensions. Parnell, though long dead, had not yet faded completely into

the shades of history. A friend, summing it up for me, referred
to the broad leather belt his uncle, who had been a docker,
used to wear. Stitched into it were three badges. They were
the Ivy Leaf, the cap badge of the Dublin Fusiliers and the
Red Hand. In time I too realised that into that belt had been
wrought the tapestry of Dublin working-class mythology.

The twenties also introduced wide-eyed childhood to two
incredible new wonders : the Talkies and the wireless. Al Jolson
in *The Singing Fool* at the La Scala (that's what everyone called
it − later it became the Capital Cinema) was an early experience of the first, while the inauguration in 1926 of Irish
Broadcasting caused domestic chaos. My father decided to
assemble our own wireless set himself. It was a crystal set with
a thing on it for tuning in to the station called 'the cat's
whiskers' and you listened in on earphones which gripped the
flesh like a vice and were an unbearable weight. Wireless
seemed an odd description. There were wires everywhere,
trailing along the floor and getting tangled about the
unfortunate dog and then trailing up walls and over pictures
and once knocking three of the mother's good cups off the
kitchen dresser. The first sound it ever picked up was, I think,
a recital by the Number One Army Band, which sounded as
though they were all playing on paper and combs. But to hear
them at all created frantic excitement.

In 1926 Larkin was again the focus of attention. A coal strike
was causing considerable hardship, especially among the poor,
so he founded some kind of Co-op which enabled him to
charter boats (he had always the ability to arrange such things
without any money) which brought coal that was sold to the
customers direct from the South Quay wall. It was fetched
home by processions of youngsters with handcarts knocked
together from pram wheels and orange boxes. I remember bare
feet and mud-spattered legs, creaking shafts and wobbling
wheels, leaden skies and rain-sodden clothes. Many of those
youngsters were permanently underfed. Tuberculosis (it was
known as consumption) was rampant and greatly feared. I
remember our terror when passing the Sanatorium on the

Pigeon House Road. It had established itself in our young imaginations as Death made manifest. People went in there and never came out. This and a wide range of other fatal and commonplace disorders implanted at an early age a nagging understanding of the frailty of the human condition and the unpredictability of all things. Death, you might say, was very noticeable.

The thirties opened up a wider range of activities. The Christian Brothers presided over education with an unrelenting emphasis on religion, nationalism and the Irish language : prayers every hour; classroom orders given mostly in Irish; punishment at the blink of an eye. The pleasant sides were football in the school grounds, plays to be rehearsed for performances at various feiseanna, and the annual Gilbert and Sullivan opera for the Christmas season. At school outings the cigarettes were dished around liberally and pupil and teacher puffed away like steam engines. The Brothers, by and large, were decent men who imposed discipline but knew the wisdom of closing the eyes now and then.

Weekends in the season often included trips to matches in Milltown, Shelbourne and Dalymount Parks. Ringsend supported Shamrock Rovers to a man ('Give it to Bob' was the chant when things were going badly). My father and his brothers followed Shelbourne but my uncle Harry played goalkeeper for Bohemians so my grandfather and my aunts were Bohemian fans. So was I, because I hero-worshipped Uncle Harry. On Saturday evenings in winter when the newsboy was heard stuffing the *Evening Mail*'s special late news sporting edition into the letterbox, the heart always missed a beat. And if Bohs had been defeated you had to hold the paper high before your face so that the aunts would not see the tears.

In 1934, which was a Holy Year, a visit with the Boy Scouts took us to Rome and Mussolini's Italy. I remember buying a funny black forage cap with the red stripe and Fascisti badge from one of their youth movement stores. We were in Spain briefly too and saw the burnt-out churches which warned of the coming civil war and the terrible future ahead for the Spanish people.

But two events of the 1930s stand out with special significance. I became a breadwinner of sorts when I landed my first job : a clerkship in the D'Olier Street office of the Dublin Gas Company at a starting salary of £1 per week. The second was a first meeting with Jim Larkin. A group of the clerks decided to join Larkin's Union if he would agree to have us, so on a sunlit evening I set off across O'Connell Bridge with a friend for Unity Hall, which stood, (or rather, staggered – it was in the last stages of decay) opposite the Pro-Cathedral. Larkin accepted us and I became a member of the Section Committee. Later I became a paid official – a Branch Secretary – with my office just beside his. When things were slack he would wander in for a chat. Once, when I told him I had proof that an employer had lied deliberately to us at a conference he refused to let me make use of it. 'Hit a man in his pocket,' he told me 'but never in his pride.' He also used to say that he didn't mind negotiating with an intelligent rogue but not an honest fool.

Then came the war and an Ireland stripped suddenly of signposts and mechanical conveyances. When we wanted to travel any distance we did so on that mainstay of Dublin life – the bicycle. The countryside, always pleasant, became wonderful for the wayfaring cyclist. There were no cars, no tourists. Only empty roads, flanked by trees, hedges, gates and fields.

What passed for simple peace and quiet in the country settled on the city like a paralysis, until the newly-founded *The Bell,* under O'Faolain's editorship, began to stir things up. O'Faolain saw officialdom and the new middle-class as representing 'Defeatism in politics, laissez-faire in social reform, a hypocritical pietism in religion . . . a class which breeds censorship, lay priests and traditionalism.'

Among those with him in the fight against this were Frank O'Connor and Peadar O'Donnell. O'Faolain accepted two of my short stories in 1942 and I made their acquaintance and later was honoured with their friendship. Mornings spent in Bewley's with Peadar O'Donnell talking and drinking coffee offered opportunities to listen to first-hand accounts of the early Trade Union Movement and the personalities (he had been with them) and politics of the 1916 period, the Troubles, the Treaty debate and the Civil War. They were as much highly informed briefing sessions on current affairs as they were discussions on the role of the Writer.

In the 1950s I began to contribute talks and short stories and eventually plays to Radio Eireann and in 1955 I joined the permanent staff as Assistant Head of Drama and Variety (the Head being Micheál O'hAodha). Here were gifted and creative men : Maurice Gorham, the Director, a man of enormous broadcasting experience; Bob O'Farachain, poet, Gaelic language expert and Thomistic scholar; Francis McManus, novelist, biographer and Head of Features; Philip Rooney, novelist and Head of Scriptwriters. Later on I moved with Philip over to television when preparations for its introduction as a national service began in 1961 and spent three months in training with the BBC. The art of scripting for television had to be mastered and the making of studio programmes and films. There were opportunities to plan shows with artists such as Jimmy O'Dea, Joe Linanne, Jack Cruise, Paddy Crosbie; to travel all over Ireland with Frank O'Connor studying under his guidance the remnants of the early Irish monastic movement, Frank's lifelong pre-occupation and love; and to meet and work with writers of international reputation.

Taking the long look back, I see a varied and gifted gallery of personalities who became friends and who were the best of company when the tasks of the day were over. It was my good fortune that my work cast my lot with theirs.

So that is a part (by no means the whole) of the accumulation of people and places and happenings which I must now contemplate in the hope of seeing in it all some recognisable pattern. It is said that we are all the offspring of our own past. I believe this to be so and I feel the attempt to harmonise it all and lay it at least to rest is going to be a long and difficult one. The gypsies have a proverb: you have to dig deep to bury your Daddy.

(1985)

Mother of Seven

The fifties, as I remember them, wore a grey face, a wan look, and a here-we-go-again air, perhaps because of the frugalities and trials of the other decades my earthly span so far had allowed me to experience: the twenties of childhood, rooted in the half-understood terrors of fratricidal hatreds and wayward assassinations; the thirties, yearning for social change and haunted by poverty: the forties, with hope wrapped-up and stored away for the war's duration and Sean Lemass, in 1943, as the nation clung on by its fingertips, summing up the position for us simply and typically: 'Our main task is to stay alive in a world where we have few friends.'

The fifties were supposed to bring in the long-awaited era of social change. As far back as December of 1942, in the middle of a world war, the Beveridge Report published in Britain had laid the foundation for hopes of social and ideological change in society's approach to the care and well-being of its citizens. It identified what it called the Five Giants in the life of man which worked for his degradation: Poverty, Disease, Ignorance, Squalor, Idleness. It laid down three principles, which were: first, the wishes of any one section of the community were not to be given undue weight as against those of other sections (a warning against Elitism); second, the determination to abolish the Five Giants nominated above; and third, to preserve individual initiative as far as possible.

All heady and idealistic stuff (one would say), easy enough

to formulate in the middle of a world war, when it was important to strengthen morale and cheer people up. But at the end of the war Britain, with its newly elected Labour government, settled down systematically and with obvious seriousness to turning the concept of the Welfare State into a reality. The idea, for its most dedicated and evangelical adherents, involved nothing less than care of the citizen from the cradle to the grave. For the more practical it meant minimum standards in income, health, housing and education.

Needless to say, the introduction just across the water of policies of comprehensive social care had its impact on the Republic also.

During the war, apart from the 50,000 or so from the Republic who had volunteered directly for war service with the British Army, some thousands more had responded to the attractions of the steady, well-paid civilian employment offered by the war effort. Now, after the war, with the setting up of the Welfare State and its manifold advantages, work in Britain became more attractive still. The outflowing stream of emigration, instead of easing off with the end of the war as had been expected, increased until it assumed crisis proportions. Between 1946 and 1951, 122,000 Irishmen and women had emigrated. From 1951 to 1956, 197,000 went. For the years 1956 to 1961 this became 212,000, well over double the pre-war figure. The pernicious effect of this exodus on a country struggling to build up its resources after six years of neutrality and commercial isolation was disturbing. Even grimmer was the likelihood that unless the flow was staunched, a time was predictable when there would be so many elderly and infirm and so few young and able-bodied remaining that the nation could grind to a halt.

Unemployment at home and the setting-up of the Welfare State in Britain were leading factors in the population crisis. But another – and one not to be ignored – was Ireland's generally low marriage rate, especially in rural parts. About this, the Bishop of Cork, the Most Rev Dr Lucey, expressed almost despairing concern: 'The rural population is vanishing and with it is vanishing the Irish race itself . . . Rural Ireland is stricken and dying and the will to marry on the land is almost gone.'

That, unquestionably, is the cry of a deeply and sincerely troubled man. But what never seemed to occur to the Bishop was that the situation regarding the sexes owed something to the attitude towards marriage and sex of his own clergy. Their fulminations against company-keeping, the actual organised spying by Holy Willies on country roads and their adjacent sin bins, the deep woods and the ditches, the surveillance of and restrictions on dancing, the pressures of official censorship on books and cinema and unofficial censorship on almost every other activity so drained Irish life of enjoyment that any young people with a bit of spunk in them at all made up their minds to get out.

Another alarmed observer was the Rev John A. O'Brien, who, noting that within the past hundred years the population of Ireland had about halved, edited a book of essays on the subject in 1954 which stimulated heated public debate and gave the phenomenon its name: *The Vanishing Irish.*

In 1949, William Norton, leader of the Labour Party in the then coalition government, urged on by his party's natural aspirations but also conscious of the likelihood of the nation bleeding to death if some attempt to bring in improved Social Welfare conditions were not made, tried to reform our own rather chaotic social insurance system. To his surprise, his efforts occasioned hierarchical disapproval.

Next came Dr Noel Browne's attempt, through his Maternal and Child Welfare Proposals (better known as his Mother and Child Scheme) to drag Irish society into the twentieth century by the hair of the head. The result: more hierarchical objections, though this time accompanied by a public outcry and with highly spectacular results – a political party smashed in bits and a government toppled. The actual objections to either Norton's or Browne's proposals proved difficult to understand at the time. By now, however, (as Montaigne might put it) persistent efforts to grasp them have managed to make them even more obscure. There were hints of State Autocracy and much tossing about of the 'principle of subsidiary function' and Article 42 of the Constitution with its guarantee 'to respect the inalienable right and duty of parents to provide, according to their means, for the religious, moral, intellectual, physical and social education of their children'. However, put in their simplest terms, it seems Norton's moves were suspected of government paternalism while Browne's seemed likely to end up with medical officers giving instruction to Catholic working-class mothers in the area of sex, a zone better left within the competence of the Bishops.

The lurid clashes over the Mother and Child scheme and the disproportionate consequences, instead of damping down the fires of debate seemed only to feed the flames. In a society where the expectations of the ordinary son of the masses could range from the achievement of a seedy kind of respectability to recruitment into the ranks of large-scale unemployment with the emigrant ship as the ultimate hope of a solution, the air began to fill with prolonged and well-orchestrated cries against the evils of a co-ordinated attempt to provide against deprivation. The tune was familiar. Here were the same oul two-and-fourpennies: Authoritarian, Obscurantist, not a lesson of any kind learned, all alive and kicking and as capable as ever of making mischief and smothering hope. In no time at all a vitriolic debate was banging away on the rights and wrongs of the Welfare State idea which was to last (almost) throughout the decade.

The Welfare State was described as 'an evil, pagan thing, stripping a man of his dignity through an outpouring of secular do-gooding'.

'Do-gooding', of course, was intended to wear a 'knitting socks for soldiers' air. It was designed to symbolise the parish work indulged in on the Sabbath by well-heeled Victorian ladies in an age when do-badding or do-nothing were the norms on the other six days of the week.

The objection was made that if the State set up a scheme which provided for a man's family in sickness it was relieving him of his right to do so himself. This, it was said, was relieving him of his basic duty and was contrary to the moral law. On the other hand, if he insured himself and his family against sickness through a commercial concern or a voluntary society, it was perfectly in order. Private insurance, it seemed, was moral. State insurance was not. There were people (otherwise sane and compassionate) who argued that the Welfare State must be resisted because it would limit the field in which those with means could exercise the virtue of charity in respect of their less-fortunate neighbours; in other words, a proportion of the population should be left in hardship so that the road to heaven might be made easier for those who were better-off.

Another opponent warned that the public mind was becoming 'permeated and obsessed by the prevailing socialist Philosophy' and that we were 'far too ready to follow the example of Britain'. 'Facilis descensus Averni', he concluded, warning us that we were stepping it out on the road to hell.

When Sean O'Faolain who edited *The Bell* and a few of us who contributed to it gave backing to the new social ideas and Noel Browne's Mother and Child Scheme, it drew down on us the wrath of the opposition, including that of Bishop Browne of Galway, who lamented these attacks on the Church, which evoked 'all the gradations of bitter hostility, hatred, or mere indifference . . . from the fury of the Orangemen of Sandy Row, to the venom of the *Irish Times* and the rancour of *The Bell*.'

'I am afraid,' O'Faolain commented in the following month's issue 'all His Lordship wants is abject compliance.'

But the voice of Religion was not entirely unanimous. One prominent debater, Father Holloway, confessed that he believed 'this understanding of a Welfare State to be deeply Christian' and to represent one of the main obstacles to Marxism raised by the English-speaking world! And others, pondering some words once spoken by Cardinal Mundelein – 'The trouble with us in the past has been that we were too often drawn into an alliance with the wrong side' – wondered was it going to happen yet again.

But by 1958 the rhetoric had cooled down a bit and indications of a change of heart were signalled in an article in the highly respected quarterly, *Studies,* which pointed out that duty to one's fellow man is not limited to what should be done for individuals: organised society was entitled to enlist government assistance where conditions warranted. The mists were clearing.

Censorship was another item which loomed large as a source of controversy in the fifties and even before. Introducing a symposium on the matter in *The Bell* in 1945, in which the contributors were Bernard Shaw, Sean O'Casey, T.C. Kingsmill Moore, James Hogan and Monk Gibbon, O'Faolain wrote:

> We now have, here, a Literary Censorship, a Film Censorship, the Censorship of the Common Law, the Censorship of the secret reports of the Librarians' Association, and the private censorship which any citizen irrespective of class, education, age, or sanity may exercise over any book in a public library merely by objecting to it.

In the matter of Literary Censorship things had become progressively more crazy. In the thirties about a hundred books were being banned annually; by the mid-fifties this figure had increased to over six hundred a year. But it was in the theatre of the fifties (where, oddly enough, no censorship officially existed) that the most outrageous events occurred.

In 1955 Cyril Cusack gave O'Casey's new play, *The Bishop's Bonfire,* its first production in the Gaiety Theatre. Rumours preceded it and ran rife in Dublin. The play was blasphemous, it was said. It was anti-clerical. O'Casey had written it as a blistering attack on religion. On opening night pickets were mounted by the religious groups while the fans queued overnight to make certain of gaining admission. As is usual in such circumstances, the protests misfired. Every other person seemed prepared to chance damnation to see the play and 1,700 people had to be turned away. The theatre packed for five weeks and would have continued to pack only the play had to give place to the Grand Opera Company which had a prior booking. In 1958 the International Theatre Festival had to be cancelled altogether when the Archbishop refused to allow the Tostal opening to be marked as usual by the celebration of a Mass because he disapproved of the plays on offer. These were *The Drums of Father Ned* by Sean O'Casey, three mime plays by Samuel Beckett, and *Bloomsday*, an adaptation of a section of Joyce's *Ulysses* by Alan McClelland.

In the previous year, Alan Simpson's and Carolyn Swift's production of Tennessee Williams' *The Rose Tattoo* ran foul of the police who declared it to be indecent and profane. Simpson was arrested and lodged in the Bridewell. Next day he was charged with having produced for gain an indecent and profane performance. The case dragged on until June 1958, when he was cleared and it was thrown out, but by then Simpson was in debt for legal costs to the tune of nearly £3,000. When he tried to recoup his losses by staging a new production the play was refused by every theatre in Dublin.

The spectre of Commmunism, I remember, haunted the fifties too. I have in front of me a circular dated 3 December 1956 and signed *An Irish Worker* which was distributed around the Dublin Fruit Markets warning the traders against the machinations of James Larkin (Junior) and the Workers' Union of Ireland. It states:

> There is a Communist Plan developed by Larkin and taught in the Russian schools for the training of Communists . . . In countries which are not favourable to Communism the party members are told to work underground through Trade Unions, Labour Parties etc. until the time arrives when they can emerge into the open and take over. James Larkin, the signer of the letter you have received studied in Moscow the whole theory and practice of Atheistic and Materialist Communism . . .

A pathological fear of Communism had haunted the new State from the start, but in the fifties it was reinforced by the waves of McCarthyism drifting across from America. In company with a small band of writers and other artists I fell

foul of this national hysteria myself. An invitation arrived in
1954 at the office of *The Bell* for a number of creative people
to visit the Soviet Union as guests of their cultural organisation
VOKS to see how life went on in their part of the world. There
were no strings attached and in January of 1955 a small party
of us set off. In the space of a few days all hell broke loose.
County Councils thrughout the country vied with each other
in passing resolutions condemning this traitorous, Godless,
Atheistical group of renegades who had gone (as one resolution
put it) 'to shake the bloodied hands of the Kremlin tyrants'.
No one bothered to enquire as to our reasons for going or
to check out our views. By the time we got back we had been
condemned by politicians and pulpit and in my own case resolutions had been passed to demand my dismissal from my job as
a Branch Secretary with the Workers' Union of Ireland. One
Saturday morning (we still used to work on Saturday mornings
in those days) I got a telephone call at the Union's office in
College Street. It was Brendan Behan. He was in the White
Horse bar on the quays and wanted to see me, so at one o'clock
I went across to join him. He told me he deplored the witch
hunt and intended to write a letter to the papers in my defence.
I was alarmed, knowing that public sympathy from a notorious
non-conformist such as Brendan would ruin me altogether. I
told him so. He begged me not to worry. He intended to sign
the letter (he said) Mother of Six. Then he looked down at his
pint-drinker's belly which protruded for several inches between
him and the counter and contemplated it for some time.

'On second thoughts,' he decided at last, 'maybe I should
make it Mother of Seven.'

In the event, the letter proved unnecessary. *The Bishop's Bonfire*
opened in the Gaiety a week later and drew the fire of the
Holy Willies away from us Russia blackguards on to the heads
of the unfortunate Cyril Cusack and Sean O'Casey. Brendan
was relieved of the necessity of deciding on the precise number
of his pregnancies.

(1986)

2

The Boy on the Back Wall

The ghosts that linger about the lanes and backways of this city have grown more numerous. Once they were from her history and the imaginations of her writers. Now they are joined by the Dead we knew and worked with, so that it is hard to walk the streets without the memory of their presence and a sense of emptiness.

Frank O'Connor was of Cork. Dublin he considered provincial. Or so he said. And when he was opposed he went further and declared it always had been. Whether he meant it or not I cannot say. It was always difficult to distinguish between a firmly held O'Connor conviction and the exuberance of Frank in full flight. I remember refusing to accept as provincial a city in which a common messenger's sense of priority inspired him to wait respectfully for Wolfe Tone the amateur music-maker to finish a sonata for two flutes before telling Wolfe Tone the conspirator that there was a warrant for his immediate arrest and to get to hell out of it. Nor a city haunted by so uncompromising a spirit as that of Jonathan Swift. Or – now that the arguments are all over and the chain is on the door – so thoughtful and discriminating a ghost as Frank O'Connor.

His presence lingers about many a street. If I associate him in a special way with the old office of *The Bell* near the GPO it is in part nostalgia for days of youth and hope but mostly for remembrances of kindnesses. I never met him there. He was a presence only in print and in occasional messages percolating down through two other benevolent autocrats of literature, Sean O'Faolain and Peadar O'Donnell. The messages were cryptic and practical. He was pushing my stories abroad; he had found me a good agent; he thought he could arrange a sojourn in the United States. I knew O'Connor's generosity long before we ever spoke a word to each other.

Eventually I met him. It was in his flat on Mespil Road, near the banks of the Grand Canal and not far from the haunts of my own childhood. I had already written about Pembroke Street and Leeson Street and the canal itself, where I walked and talked with Frank the odd time on long summer evenings. There is a quality about that stretch of the canal between Leeson Street and Baggot Street, a greenness, a tranquillity, an ineffable pensiveness. Dogs nose along the grassy banks or bob out suddenly with sticks between their teeth; children on the narrow planks of the lock gates offer their bright young lives hourly to the raging whirlpools below; old men, by repetition reassured I suppose, smoke their pipes and look on placidly; goats used to graze there too – whoever owned them. And yet it was always quiet and timeless, as though the children and the dogs, the old man and the goats and the crashing waters existed only on canvas. I think Frank fell in love with it too. He had memories of it from his first youthful sojourn in Dublin, the time he lived on Pembroke Road, existing on a diet of coffee and buns which he got in Bewleys, because he was as yet too shy to venture into the more forbidding and formal restaurants. When he died he was living in a flat at the Baggot Street end, where his window provided a frame which allowed him, as it were, to hang the canal masterpiece on his study wall. That was where I last spoke with him. I left him seated at his desk, the canal masterpiece in front of him, a script before him, his thoughts bent inwards, the sunlight falling on the high forehead and abstracted face, the writer and the living painting forever inseparable. The penniless and unknown young man of nearly fifty years before was now Dr O'Connor, the most highly regarded of Irish writers. Like his own beloved seventh-century monk he wrote well under his greenwood tree, and like him too, he had found where he belonged.

But how long had it taken him to get there? And through what unacknowledged agonies of insult and isolation? He was never one to wallow in early misfortunes or pursue personal grudge against the inequalities of society. On the contrary. He was very much his own man, self-sufficient and assertive. Unbruised, you would think. Those he disliked he treated with a medieval disdain; if he grew argumentative and slightly impossible when he was with you it meant he held you in warm affection. Most of his literary work, rooted in his own experiences of childhood and early youth, that small store of material which is virtually all a good writer can ever draw on (after twenty or so, nothing much happens), reflects him as I knew him. Sardonic, iconoclastic, rippling with poised and quizzical comedy.

Yet his early life, from which the material was drawn, was lonely, obscure and practically penniless. Avid for scholarship, his education was (by his own account) hardly worth mentioning. In an environment of ignorance and hopelessness aspiration goaded him until the back lanes of Cork were made bearable only because his gift of fantasy could banish them altogether for long stretches at a time.

> I was always very fond of heights and afterwards it struck me that reading was only another form of height, and a more perilous one . . . I climbed the door of the outhouse and up the roof to the top of the wall. It was on a level with the respectable terrace behind ours, which had front gardens and a fine view, and I often sat there for hours on terms of relative equality with the policeman in the first house who dug close beside me and gave me ugly looks but could not think up a law to keep me from sitting on my own back wall.

But when he came down from the wall to seek companionship above his station, though it was only that of the slightly bigger lanes, he found the bigger, like the policeman, spurning the smaller. Even in the matter of lanes, tuppence ha'penny would have no truck with tuppence. His defence for a while was to devour stories of English public school life, identifying himself with chaps who didn't peach on a pal and whose uncles bestowed fivers on well-thought-of nephews for midnight beanos in the dormitories. There was always the possibility, he felt, that if he kept reading about expensive schooling some of the education might rub off. And for a time he invented for himself the fiction that he was some sort of highborn changeling and that his father and mother were not his real parents at all.

But then, the job of growing up in any generation in Ireland has always required concentration and skill and those of us who manage to stick it out eventually reach a point in life when we pause to consider how. In my own schooldays, apart from the perennial circumstances of poverty, the political situation was the hazard. As I remember it, this came to a head on Remembrance Day, when the fathers of some of us put on their service medals and marched and afterwards gathered in the pubs to congratulate each other on the helping hand they had given to Catholic Belgium and the freedom of small nations. Simultaneously, the fathers of the other crowd gathered in other pubs to declare once again that they served neither King nor Kaiser but Ireland and offered to prove it by showing their War of Independence wounds to all and sundry. Remembrance Day always led to bloody conflicts among us kids in the school yard, with each of us wearing either a lily or a poppy (ones improvised out of sweet wrappers), depending on where the father had been during those difficult years and whether you liked him sufficiently to uphold his ideological commitments to the point of certain assault and possible martyrdom. There were a few pacifists, of course, whose oul fellas had had the good sense to stay under the bed, but I don't think either side had much time for these.

The world Frank grew up in, which sowed the seeds of all this, posed its own version of the vexed Irish question. His father was an ex-British soldier with a disability pension and

a fear that political activities of a disaffected hue might lose
it for him. O'Connor's teacher, on the other hand, the one
who rescued him from the intellectual vacuum of the forgotten
streets, was a nationalist of intellect and intensity who spread
disloyalty to the Empire by every means to hand. His singing
classes resounded with songs that were sweet, but seditious.
The beauties of English poetry he conveyed through lines such
as those of Walter Scott:

> Breathes there a man with soul so dead
> Who never to himself has said:
> This is my own, my native land!
> (with a hissing emphasis on the last line).

He also wrote on the blackboard, much to the astonishment
of a headmaster who regarded himself as the Crown's Own
Henchman, the first sentence in the Irish language that most
of his class had ever seen: 'Waken your courage – Ireland'.

Perhaps it has always been better to be poor and oppressed
than simply poor. In the Ireland of O'Connor's youth
oppression provided food for the spirit and the intellect at least.
It created a class within society whose members were bound
together by their capacity for idealism and not by equality
of family profession or income. One of the few acceptable
legacies of the period is that in Ireland today a man's
intellectual interests will admit him to the company he desires,
regardless of his social background. But the initial obstacles
of a poverty-ridden childhood he must still engage and
overcome with what tender weapons he can muster.

Corkery opened a window for O'Connor on the world he
had craved, where literature and music and intellectual
company were at last accessible. He set him on the road to
learning, which he travelled still in poverty but now at least
with a sense of direction and purpose. As a teacher of Irish
he became one of the brigade of revivalists who at that time
were pedalling with devoted zeal down the rough roads of
Ireland, teaching her ancient language in dreary halls and
lamplit kitchens, stirring again her pride in her ancient past,

proclaiming her glory and her right to be free. In my own growing-up time the original zeal had got very much out of hand, with the result that it had become the fashion to laugh at the patriotic excesses of the fierce, fáinne-decorated men in tweeds and bicycle clips. I confess I did my share of it and joined in with gusto. God knows, some of them earned it: they were fanatical Sean the Baptists, full of spittle and sunburstry, driven demented, it always seemed to me, by the inner naggings of incessant little Celtic demons. But, by and large, they were good men who deserved better.

The Movement brought O'Connor out of the city and into the little cottages of the countryside at an age when he was young enough to absorb the experience creatively. It gave him something to belong to as of birthright, a past which lived in literature and ancient stone. Here, he himself decided, was something to be dignified about and he venerated that past and studied it all his life. The Movement also involved him in the tragedy of the Civil War, an unhappy if unavoidable title for a conflict of fratricidal brutality and ruthlessness. His period of active service was brought to an end by capture and imprisonment, which in turn provided the time for reading, study and eventually a dispassionate acceptance of the disastrous collapse of the Ideal. When he arrived home after his release his mother, whom he adored, looked long at him and said, suddenly bursting into tears:: 'It has made a man of you'. It had done something in addition to that. It had made a writer of him.

All that was thirty years behind him when I first met him. The experiences of childhood and youth, of war and disillusion, had found expression through short stories which earned him an international reputation; his love of the past had been lavished on translations, some of them exquisite pieces in their own right, that covered over a thousand years of Irish poetry. In addition he had lived through the experience of being made something of a pariah by the State he had helped to create. Irish society in the thirty years between the twenties and the fifties of the present century provided an extraordinary spectacle. A fierce puritanism out of all harmony with the traditional laxity of Irish ways took hold of the new State. Politicians, once excommunicated for taking arms against British rule, as were the Fenians before them, now vied with each other in public pietism. Republicans meant it when they referred to the Bishops as Princes of the Church. Crossroad céilís were forbidden and dancing generally was restricted. Company-keeping in particular was discouraged. The chairman of practically every local committee was the parish priest or one of his curates. A book censorship Board of the most bigoted kind was set up with such effect that every reputable Irish writer of the period was banned. Sean O'Faolain was denounced as an anti-cleric, Peadar O'Donnell as a Communist and Frank himself, the third of *The Bell* trio, had his translation of Merriman's classic Irish Poem, *The Midnight Court,* prohibited. Older writers were not immune. O'Casey, who replied by making uproarious farces out of the situation, was regarded as a cross between a renegade and an anti-Christ; Joyce was unmentionable but had already made his answer:

> O Ireland my first and only love
> Where Christ and Caesar are hand in glove.

Except that it was not Christ at all but some phrenetic misrepresentation.

I remember, as recently as 1951, the Bishop of Galway warning the Association of Catholic University Students against the 'gradations of bitter hostility to the Church, which ranged from the fury of the Orangemen of Sandy Row, to the venom of the *Irish Times* and the rancour of *The Bell*'. Needless to say, O'Faolain and O'Donnell and O'Connor replied, with some assistance now from those of us who were learning to lisp in their numbers; but for Frank to be banned for his work in the cause of Gaelic civilisation and lumped in with the Orangemen of Sandy Row, must have been a bitter pill to swallow, especially when administered by a representative of the ex-communicators.

Yet his real fury was loosed not on his own behalf but in

defence of one unskilled in argument and unprotected by eminence and learning: the old tailor of Gougane Barra, whose fireside talk, full of the old Irish tradition and folklore, was collected in book form by Eric Cross and later banned for being 'in its general tendency indecent'. This was followed by the arrival one day of three priests. They entered the cabin of the tailor and his wife and, determined to make an example of them for the community at large, forced the old man to go down on his knees and burn his own copy of the book. Later, when the Censorship Appeals Board was set up, it was decided officially that the book was not indecent after all and might safely be put into the hands of anybody. But the old man and his wife had suffered for their sins by then and were both dead. And Frank, himself a dedicated lover of folk talk and folk ways, wrote: 'One lesson it taught me, and others too, I think: that it would be far better that the language and traditions of Ireland should go into the grave with that great-hearted couple than that we should surrender our children to the professors and priests and folklorists.' There are signs that forty years of obscurantism and stubborn clerical casuistry may be coming to an end, for books are being unbanned now and young priests are being instructed at ordination to abandon paternalism in favour of dialogue. We make progress, I hope. But what single one among the crozier-shakers, so assured of being the henchmen of God, can stick his head for half a minute into heaven to say to the dead: 'Sorry, oul son, it was all a bit of a misunderstanding'?

I remember a few summers ago, travelling around Ireland with Frank for a television programme on monasteries and monasticism, having difficulty in persuading him to visit Inchcleraun in Lough Ree.

'I've always been a bit afraid of islands,' he explained.

'But you're living on an island.'

'I know bloody well I am,' he said feelingly. And no wonder. But he came eventually and we spent the day examining the remains of the six churches which had sprung up around St Diarmuid's sixth century settlement. Then there was the long trip back to Athlone, with someone making tea in the galley, the surface of the lake calm and one of those everstretching, heartbreakingly beautiful evenings lingering above us. Through the trees, where the island was slipping away behind us, we could see the ruined walls and empty windows of the churches. I listened to Frank quoting:

> Grant me sweet Christ, the grace to find –
> Son of the Living God –
> A small hut in a lonesome spot
> To make it my abode
>
> A little pool, but very clear
> To stand beside the place
> Where all men's sins are washed away
> By sanctifying grace
>
> A southern aspect for the heat
> A stream along its foot
> A smooth green lawn with rich top soil
> Propitious to all fruit

He stopped and said:

'What are you smiling at?'

'I was thinking of St Anthony, the Anchorite of Coma,' I said, 'who spent several years in the desert, weaving mats and wrestling with demons.'

'You're a damned Joyce man,' Frank said, 'you must learn to dream.'

But I knew how to dream. Almost every Irishman does. It is something that saves us in the heel of the hunt, no matter what Shaw may have said about it.

'I was applying the brake,' I explained. 'You do it yourself.'

It is a trick you work out for yourself or pick up from others. Frank found it on his release from prison, while still in his early youth. Underprivilege, insult, rejection and longing he had fought first with dreaming. Then he called on his acquired reserves of cynicism and with this combination created from unpromising material a style vibrant with gaiety and a philosophy which viewed the misadventures and conceits of mankind as essentially comic. The mixture was evident in his mature personality, in his veneration for the nobility of Ireland's past and his mockery of her ignoble present. He was a patriot who found it impossible over long periods to put up with life in Ireland – which is not at all unusual – and an iconoclast who spent his closing years campaigning to preserve the monuments of his country from destruction – which is rather more so.

Vanity he had in plenty: it had helped him to survive. Self-pity, none. He was too disciplined a craftsman to allow it to escape into his work and (although it must sometimes have darkened his private moments) too wise to indulge a weakness that might destroy him as a man. And when he died he had not yet had time to say all that was in him to say. The autobiography was not so much a last word as a re-examination, in preparation for a new attempt on the mysterious processes of literary creation. Or so I believe. I remember making Frank laugh once by telling him about an old man I once knew, notorious in this city where such things are not much regarded for ending each day in a self-contained miasma of alcohol. When he died, although it was well known that he never attended church, chapel or meetinghouse, his widow assured me that he was a deeply religious man and that he prayed at the fire each night for all his departed friends by naming them aloud and cracking each finger joint in turn. It was one way of doing it, we agreed, and as good a way as any.

Then, I suppose, we talked of something else.

(1969)

Salud

My first encounter with Peadar O'Donnell was *Islanders*, that unforgettable picture of Donegal life which I read at the age of fifteen or thereabouts. It was deeply moving, so much so that I left it lying around to impress an elderly relative, a Donegal woman herself, who was staying with us at the time. She picked it up eventually but the effect was unexpected, a sort of genteel yelp.

'Merciful God, child,' she said, 'you shouldn't be reading Peadar O'Donnell. That man is a Communist.' A few years later, when I was drinking coffee with the Red Menace in person, Peadar valued the remark as a useful sample of current literary criticism.

That was in Bewley's of Westmoreland Street, where it was Peadar's custom to hold court during his editor-of-*The Bell* days. He was in his fifties then, a determined, lively and talkative man with a mane of silver grey hair and a corduroy jacket which was unusual at the time and, in its unorthodox way, distinguished. You were likely to find him there most mornings, occasionally with the big guns – O'Faolain or O'Flaherty or O'Connor – but more usually with up-and-coming young men, such as Tony Cronin or John Montague or Brendan Behan. If there was an air of unusual commotion as you entered, you probably guessed that Paddy Kavanagh was present.

Peadar, of course, did most of the talking, about general subjects that were forever dear to him, such as the need to develop the fishing industry or the problems of the west; or matters of the moment, the attack on O'Faolain for his essay on *The Vanishing Irish* or Paul Blanchard's book on Irish Catholicism, which Peadar found sincere, fair-minded and wrong; or simply his unfailing curiosity and concern about people and his memories of far-off Donegal. He described how the people of Glenmore, for instance, received the news of the declaration of war between Russia and Japan at the beginning of the century. They remembered the effect of the Boer War a few years previously on the price of wool, so they consulted the schoolmaster and the widely travelled Tayman on the present possibilities. When the schoolmaster coughed and bemoaned his bad chest, it was the signal to put the poteen bottle on the table, which they did.

'There now,' said the man of the house, 'look after your chest. And look after the Tayman's chest while you're at it.'

Then the master marked out various places on the gable and measured in handspans for their benefit and information the distance between Japan and Glenmore.

The Bell, Peadar will have it, and indeed rightly, was first and last O'Faolain's achievement. Nevertheless, he himself played his unique part, sometimes in unorthodox ways, such as his scheme to supply litter boxes to the Corporation free, provided *The Bell* could rent the space on them to various advertisers and keep itself shakily solvent on the proceeds. Money was always a problem with *The Bell* and Peadar was the one who found the solutions, usually through his influence with anonymous contacts in the capitalist world he was more or less dedicated to overthrow. He had his own editorial style too, so that during his period of editorship *The Bell* changed a bit in personality, not so much in the field it covered, but in its manner of covering it. He had the ability, when he put his mind to it, to get an intelligent and informative contribution out of the most unpromising and apparently ungifted source, mainly through meeting and talking and prodding a mind into unfamiliar activity. O'Faolain's *Bell* reflected his own sharp-sightedness and polemical skill. With the height of good manners it could poleaxe an opponent and its characteristics were courage (rare in those days) and intellectual muscle. Peadar's had another kind of strength – physical muscle, perhaps, if that will serve at all adequately to describe his habit of testing theory against life and his concern to encourage his writers to dig more deeply into the thought patterns of people in their ordinary environment for aspects of that elusive article: Irish Reality. People, he believed, possessed that Truth as a natural heritage and for Peadar, as for James Connolly, Ireland without its people meant nothing more than the oft-quoted 'combination of chemical elements'. He cottoned on early to the determination of middle-class revolutionaries to keep Connolly's working-class aspirations securely buried with him in the grave. His resolve to resurrect and nourish them drew him into the trade union movement, the War of Independence and the Civil War.

It began in Donegal when he was a young teacher on the island of Arranmore at a time when the islanders were making ready for the annual journey to Scotland to gather the potato harvest. Word came from one source that there was a strike in the potato fields, followed by a denial from Scotland and advice that they should travel. Earnings from potato harvesting were an important part of island economy so Peadar decided to go over to sort things out. The experience lit up his world and moulded his life. In Glasgow he met leaders such as Manny Shinwell and Willie Gallagher and got interested in the working-class struggle and socialism. In the tattie fields he slept beside the immigrant harvest workers:

> I bedded down on straw, under musty army blankets, resenting everything around me, even angry with the workers for being so passive in face of such conditions. And then one sleepness night with men and women, boys and girls, family groups asleep around me, my imagination kindled and, in those people who came close to me as my own breath, I saw a remnant of the Irish of history, heroically holding on to homes in Ireland.

His allegiance remained there. He joined the Irish Transport and General Workers Union because of it and in the War of Independence and the Civil War his concern was not for dictionary republics but a country conscious of the needs of all its people.

Peadar neither drinks nor smokes but the air of his native Donegal goes to his head like a glass of whiskey. Or, more accurately, to his heart. I've been there with him a couple of times, to the house he was born in outside Dungloe where the fiddle his father once played still hangs on the wall; to the glen in which he was wounded and cared for; to the still busy island of Arranmore and the deserted little island of Iniskeeragh which provided the setting for *Islanders*. We went to Glenveigh which as commander of an IRA service unit he occupied during the War of Independence. He told me he had instructions to burn it but didn't, and as we stood looking at it together an untypical silence fell, which puzzled me until he broke it:

'I'm wondering did I do the wrong thing,' he said. He seemed to mean it.

As to his books, he has always played down his role as writer, though the list is impressive: *Storm; Islanders; Adrigoole; The Knife; On the Edge of the Stream; The Gates Flew Open; Salud! an Irishman in Spain; There Will Be Another Day; The Big Windows*. It proves that he has been as consistently the author as the man of action. 'Everybody accumulates experience,' he has said, 'those with sharp eyes and sharp ears more than their share.' While in prison he remembered fishing as a child with his father, starting so as to be on the fishing grounds of Iniskeeragh by dawn. The impact of that memory triggered off the mysterious process. 'I stepped,' he said, 'through one of those dawns into a book: *Islanders*.' It reminds one of Joyce's remark: 'What is imagination, but memory'.

Peadar has always had it in abundance. Enormous courage too. And compassion. And humour of the droll Donegal brand. We passed a house where two old ladies had lived who had once given him a kitten.

'I must have been very small at the time,' he said, 'and that kitten had reached about its fifth generation when they were still enquiring, any time I met them, how the kitten was doing.'

The story is simple. For me the magic is how the old ladies come alive for a brief instant. That has been Peadar's gift through a rich lifetime, one that has refreshed his friends and borne up himself through the good times and the bad.

(1973)

Published as a tribute to Peadar O'Donnell on the occasion of his 80th birthday.

The Minstrel Boy

Francis Ledwidge was born on 19 August 1887, the eighth child in the family of Patrick and Anne Ledwidge. His father was a migrant labourer, his mother – formerly Anne Lynch – a native of Slane, the little village on the banks of the Boyne some eight miles from Navan and nine from Drogheda. The family home was a neat Council cottage at Janeville, about a quarter of a mile from the village along the Drogheda road.

When Francis was five his father died, leaving the mother to fend for her young family by doing seasonal work for farmers at a rate of two shillings and sixpence a day, or – when that was not available – by taking in washing, knitting socks and doing mending for neighbours and their families.

In these circumstances, in spite of his exceptional brightness and intelligence, the boy had to leave school at fourteen to take work with a local farmer. Even at that early age he was making verses and scribbling them down on whatever came to hand: in one instance, which still survives, the wall of a cowbyre. At fifteen he was apprenticed to a grocer in Drogheda and a short while later he went to similar work in a shop in Rathfarnham, then a suburb of Dublin. The city proved so unbearable to him, however, and the pull of home so irresistible, that after a few days he crept out of the house when all were asleep and walked the thirty miles home through the night. His mother received him without reproach.

Work as a roadmender and as a ganger followed. In 1912

he became secretary of the Slane Branch of the Meath Labour Union and carried on its business from a rented office in The Square, Navan. When war came in 1914 he was serving also as a member of the Navan Board of Guardians where, as in the rest of the country, there were divided opinions as to the course Ireland should follow. As is usual in Ireland with such institutions and in such situations, there was much passing and rescinding of resolutions, a procedure which taxed the patience of the young Ledwidge. The older men sided with John Redmond and backed the recruiting campaign. Ledwidge disagreed and favoured the Sinn Fein stand of MacEoin and Pearse. In the heated debate that followed it was hinted that his attitude had roots not in principle but in personal cowardice and the innuendo rankled. After some days of painful reflection he presented himself at Richmond Barracks in Dublin and enlisted with the Royal Enniskilling Fusiliers. Later he was to say: 'I joined the British Army because she stood between Ireland and an enemy common to our civilization and I would not have her say that she defended us while we did nothing at home except pass resolutions.' The date of his decision was 24 October 1914.

It may well have been influenced also by a broken love affair. While he was a ganger on the roads Ledwidge fell in love with a slender, brown-haired girl from Slane, Ellie Vaughey. He was twenty-six, she twenty. She returned his love and they met and walked together for some months, until Ellie's relatives persuaded her to break it off. A match between a road ganger and a girl whose family owned a substantial parcel of land was considered unsuitable. It was difficult for both of them but Ellie conformed with the conventional outlook of the times. Later she married a local boy who was considered more suitable. They went to live in Manchester where Ellie died in June 1915. Ledwidge never shook off his grief at their parting and her subsequent death. Many of his poems make reference to their courtship and his loss.

His enlistment also coincided with a period when a career of outstanding literary promise was beginning to open up to him. The childhood habit of making rhymes had developed with his increasing awareness of people and nature. Even while working on the roads he would read his verses for the entertainment of his workmates whenever bad weather obliged them to leave off and take shelter. On one such occasion they removed the poem from his overcoat pocket afterwards and, unknown to him, sent it off to the *Drogheda Independent,* where it was subsequently published. It was his first appearance in print and the cause of much pride and excitement among his mates. But interest in a far more influential quarter was to follow.

In 1912, on the advice of a friend, he had sent his notebook of poems to Lord Dunsany at Dunsany Castle, also in Meath. Dunsany, himself a writer, was deeply impressed by the fresh and lyric quality of the verses and wrote: 'I was astonished by the brilliance of that eye that had looked at the fields of Meath and seen there all the simple birds and flowers with a vividness that made those pages like a magnifying glass through which one looked at familiar things seen thus for the first time. . . .'

A friendship based on their common regard for literature soon began between the two men, from worlds then unthinkably apart in terms of social caste, political allegiance and religious belief. Ledwidge was befriended and given full access to Dunsany Castle, its library especially, while Dunsany became patron and advocate, offering critical advice, collecting the poems and seeking a publisher.

Ledwidge's period of active service began with the 10th Division at Gallipoli in August 1915. When they were finally evacuated from the beaches in December of that year 19,000 of his comrades of the 10th Division were left behind, dead. There followed freezing winter months on the Greco-Serbian border, through which Ledwidge continued to write poetry whenever opportunity offered and, when it was possible, to send them back to Dunsany for assessment and safe-keeping. But long months of active service, short rations, rain, snow and storm and then the painful retreat from the mountains back to Salonika had seriously undermined his health. The poems he had managed to write suffered too. 'I have many [new poems] in my haversack,' he wrote from hospital in

Salonika, 'all faded with Balkan rains.' He was still in hospital when *Songs of the Fields* reached him, his first published book. It won glowing notices from reviewers and ran to three editions. Meanwhile Dunsany was busy selecting poems for the next.

Ledwidge got home on leave in May of 1916, a fortnight or so after the Easter Rising. In Dublin the rubble of O'Connell Street still smouldered and the executions had shocked a public that up to then had been unsympathetic to the rebels. Ledwidge's backing of the ideals of the leaders had led to his fateful clash with the Navan Board of Guardians in 1914. Now his admiration for those executed, particularly for Thomas MacDonagh with whom he had been friendly, divided his heart and allegiance. Yet when it was suggested to him in Slane that he should desert and join 'the hill men', in other words the men on the run who would band together later to fight the British occupation of Ireland until freedom had been won, he refused. The numberless deaths of cherished comrades he had already witnessed made that role impossible.

On 26 December 1916 he crossed the Channel on his way to the Western Front and the last and terrible battle of Yprès. Through weeks of vile weather and incessant bombardment his thoughts dwelt constantly on home. 'Death is as interesting to me as life,' he wrote to Katherine Tynan in January 1917. 'I have seen so much of it from Suvla to Serbia and now in France. I am always homesick. I hear the roads calling, and the hills, and the rivers wondering where I am. It is terrible to be always homesick.'

Thoughts of home meant also thoughts of old and dear friends and, in particular, thoughts of Ellie. In May or June of the same year he had so vivid a dream of her that he wrote of it to Dunsay in a letter when enclosing one of his poems, and wondered if it was a portent of his death.

Meanwhile preparations for the all-out assault were coming to a head. Heavy rain began and continued incessantly through the last week of July, churning the ground into a swamp, so that heavy planks had to be bolted together to make a road for the advance of men and guns. On 31 July, while the assault was taking place, Ledwidge was engaged all day in the road-laying which had to continue in spite of heavy shelling. In the evening, weary and drenched by the rain, they were snatching a break to gulp down their issue of tea when a shell burst beside them, killing seven and wounding twelve. Ledwidge was among the seven. It was a day of terrible slaughter. The assault claimed the lives of 135,000 men. The ground gained was a hundred yards.

Three months after his death his second volume of poems, *Songs of Peace,* was published and some months later his third, *Last Songs.*

In the years following the end of the war Georgian poetry went out of fashion and was replaced by the anti-romantic, anti-pastoral idiom introduced by Eliot and adopted by the Auden-Isherwood school. Ledwidge, however, continued to attract interest and held his poet's place. His complete poems were published in 1919. Due to the painstaking research of his biographer, Alice Curtayne, these were added to extensively in the new *Complete Poems* edited by her and published again in 1974.

He has been referred to variously as The Poet of the Boyne, The Blackbird of Slane, The Scavenger Poet and The Hero Poet. They were all titles of condescension, however well-meaning they were intended to be. Ledwidge was a consummate craftsman, an accurate observer of nature and the human heart and a skilled shaper of verse which retains its freshness and its simplicity. There is much in it of the Gaelic tradition and everything in it of his native County Meath. In a word, he is an Irish poet and likely to hold his place as such as long as anthologies of Irish poetry continue to be published.

He is buried in the second plot of Artillery Wood cemetery, near the village of Boesinghe in Belgium. A plaque on the bridge over the Boyne at Slane commemorates him.

(1976)

I acknowledge with gratitude my indebtedness to Alice Curtayne for the biographical facts of the poet's short life. They are to be found in her biography: *Francis Ledwidge: A Life of the Poet* published by Martin, Brian & O'Keeffe.

Dear Harp of My Country

Thomas Moore was born at No 12 Aungier Street, Dublin, on 27 May 1779, in a room above his father's grocer's shop. As might be expected, the family resources were modest. His first musical efforts were airs picked out with one finger on a harpsichord surrendered by a customer in part payment of a debt. His sleeping quarters consisted of a partitioned-off corner of the bedroom which circumstances compelled him to share with his father's two young shop assistants who were serving their apprenticeship to the trade. Despite the lessons in polite usage from an elderly gentlelady which his anxious mother managed to arrange and attendance at Samuel Whyte's Academy in Grafton Street where Sheridan the dramatist had once been a pupil, these were lowly beginnings for one who would later be hailed by his contemporaries as a poet of the highest rank and whose singing was to dominate the country houses of the aristocracy and the salons of fashionable London throughout the first thirty or forty years of the nineteenth century.

Yet so it was to be. And Tom Moore was to stand as high with his fellow poets as he would with fashion. Keats wrote of him: 'I like that man.' Shelley sought his good opinion. Sir Walter Scott declared eternal friendship. Lord Byron named him as one of the two men he had ever truly liked and entrusted the editing of his memoirs to him. Only Wordsworth who, to be fair about it, had already given clear warning that any nymphs, shepherdesses, cupids, crystal fountains or similar elegant whimsicalities found loitering with intent in the sacred groves of Inspiration would be shot at sight, had the hard word to say: 'It is very pretty, Mr Moore, but it is not poetry.'

To which Moore, in regard to his *Irish Melodies* at least, could have answered: 'Mr Wordsworth, I have already said so.'

And he had – in his preface to the third volume:

> With respect to the verses which I have written for these melodies, as they are intended rather to be sung than read, I can answer for their sound with somewhat more confidence than for their sense.

The young Tom Moore's home life was entirely happy. With his sisters the bond was deeply affectionate and remained so to the end. His father, in all that affected his family, was kindly, tolerant and easygoing. His mother simply doted on him and he on her. While she lived he wrote to her weekly – and sometimes twice in the week – to tell her all that had happened or that he hoped would happen. No success was too dazzling to tempt the slightest neglect. Her happiness was his deepest concern; his welfare, hers.

Anastasia Moore was young, kindhearted and musical. Her pleasure was to have friends to supper and musical evenings. They were gay parties, the more so for being overcrowded. Solos and duets were sung, piano pieces rendered, an officer of the Irish Brigade added a romantic touch on occasion by obliging on the Spanish guitar. Anastasia's favourite song was 'How Sweet in the Woodlands,' which suited her very pleasant voice. Young Tom followed his mother. Jack Moore remained content to look on. More than content. His feelings are echoed in a little sentence in a long letter he wrote to Tom many years later: '. . . surely no parents had ever such happiness in a child.'

Politics, however, took him differently. Mysterious visitors in the green and forbidden uniform of the National Guard were sometimes to be seen at his table. The Moores were Catholics and wanted an end to legal discrimination. They were fully behind a parliament in Ireland for the people of

Ireland and shared in the political battles of the times. When Grattan and Fitzgerald were returned to parliament in the election of 1790 and passed in triumphant procession down Aungier Street, Jack Moore placed the young Tom by him in the top window to wave a bunch of laurel and to do so with such enthusiasm that the family were satisfied he had caught Grattan's eye. On another occasion he took the child to a public dinner in honour of Napper Tandy and could report on his return that the great man had taken young Tom on his knee and kept him there for several minutes.

These were heady days when it seemed that the yoke of oppression might soon be removed – perhaps altogether. But hopes faded in the welter of executions that followed the Rising of 1798 and died completely with Emmet's failure and execution five years later. Some of those who died had been friends of Tom's in his student days at Trinity. Their memory and their tragedy are echoed in the most haunting of his Irish melodies, the project which represents the crowning point of his career.

Moore had gone to London in 1799 destined, so his parents believed (who had scraped and pinched to provide him with the opportunity) for the Bar. Tom had other hopes. With him he had his translation of the *Odes of Anacreon* and a selection of poems which he had been writing since the age of fifteen. Both found a publisher and enjoyed success. Meanwhile, through the patronage of Lord Moira, a man of liberal views, he had become known in the fashionable houses and was building up a high reputation as a singer. At his first appearance before an exalted audience his lack of inches and chubby appearance as he walked to the piano drew (so an eye-witness tells us) 'a contemptuous titter'. But when he began to sing a deep silence descended and his listeners were spellbound. The seal was put to his gift as a performer by a happy chance.

Edward Bunting had spent a number of years collecting the music of the Irish people from harpers and singers in the remotest parts of the country, a heritage which threatened to be lost forever as the native language and the profession of wandering musician declined. A Dublin publisher, William Power, suggested to Moore during one of his visits home that he should provide verses to match a selection of the airs and collaborate with Sir John Stevenson in arranging them for voice and piano. Moore recognised the worth of the suggestion and began work almost immediately. The first collection was issued in 1808 and others, ten in all, followed, the last appearing in 1834. They were instantly successful, so much so that Tom was able to turn his attention to another matter.

In 1809, while taking part in a run of amateur theatricals in Kilkenny, he met a Miss E. Dyke. On 25 March 1811, Tom and Bessie Dyke were married. On this occasion, probably the only time in his life, Tom failed to keep his mother up to date. Bessie was an actress. She was sixteen and just half his age. She was very beautiful. She was also penniless. Heads shook and tongues wagged. They might not have troubled. Bessie remained for the length of their days a sweet-natured wife, a lively companion, a capable housewife, a thrifty manager, a perfect mother. And when they got over their fright the Moores took Bessie to their always tender hearts. Tom loved Bessie to the end of his days.

Tom Moore turned out other highly successful work in the course of his life, but nothing to endure as did the *Irish Melodies*. They were unique not only for the beauty of the airs and their felicitous lyrics but because of Moore's display of technical mastery in the selection and ordering of words which made them eminently singable, endowing them with qualities of such singular clarity and immediacy that they captivated the ear and the emotions of the listener. The sentiment was delicately evoked, the manner was inimitable. London relished the unexpected element of Irish nationalism, the brooding sorrow and muted aspiration of a people in chains. For Dublin – and ultimately for Ireland at large – it was their mingling of ancient pride and recent sorrows, their fusing of kings of old and heroes of the present: Brian in his glory, Emmet on his gallows, Jack Moore and the bunch of laurel, Napper Tandy and the child on his knee, the walks in the country and the spectre of Emmet's lonely sacrifice – all that 'delirium of the brave', as a far greater poet put it – remained to trouble the deeper consciousness of Tom Moore and to bathe recollection in its uneasy light. Whatever the critics might say – and they said a lot – about Tom's mistreatment of the native melodies, about his hobnobbing with lords and ladies, about the nature of his patriotism, he was still the National Poet, enshrined in many a green-bound volume in countless Irish houses and sung with emotion and pride at every musical evening. An anonymous journalist got it exactly when he wrote, in 1810: 'Moore has done more for the revival of our national spirit than all the political writers Ireland has seen for a century.'

Latterly Tom Moore has suffered an eclipse. But for over a hundred years he was Poet Laureate of Ireland by popular assent. Thereafter his presence was spread throughout Irish life and literature; not necessarily in the forefront, but in those allusions and undercurrents that are the heart of the matter. He was the glow of sentiment at weddings and gatherings; the song in childish voices spilling over from classrooms into listening streets; the quotation that formed of itself in a moment of unexpected recollection; the echo that wandered always in the deeps of the emigrant's heart.

(1977)

The Offering of Swans

There is a poem by an Irish poet in which he sees his spirit slipping away from his sleeping body to visit the place of its greatest happiness:

> No easeful meadows nor delightful springs
> Nor visionary islands lure it best,
> But far off on the margin of the West
> A seagrey house whereby the blackbird sings.

The seagrey house was Renvyle House in County Galway and the poet Oliver St John Gogarty, who was born in Dublin in 1878. He also owned a house on the island in Tully Lake and, on his death in New York, his body was brought back at his own request for burial in Ballynakill Churchyard. In addition to these physical reminders of Gogarty's deep affection for the countryside around Renvyle, his regard is recorded time and again in both his poems and his prose works. He drove down there whenever his private and public duties permitted, usually in the company of celebrated eccentrics of the period or prominent figures of the Irish Literary Revival and after 1923, when his house was deliberately burned down by anti-Treaty forces, he lamented bitterly the destruction of 'the long, low house in the ultimate land of the undiscovered West. I remember the giant fuchsia bush, spreading like a banyan tree on the garden path blinded by its growth. . . .'

Oliver St John Gogarty, who was born at 5 Rutland (now

Parnell) Square, Dublin, was a man of achievement in many different fields. As a young student he became both a champion cyclist and an acknowledged wit, the author, according to the writer George Moore, 'of all the limericks that enable us to live in Dublin.' He was on intimate terms with the leading figures of his age, among them Arthur Griffith and Michael Collins, W.B. Yeats and James Joyce, George Russell, Lord Dunsany and Augustus John. He was also a distinguished physician with a fine reputation as a specialist in ear, nose and throat surgery. He became a Senator in the first Senate of the Irish Free State and was a qualified air pilot. But perhaps his proudest achievement was in November 1936, when Yeats selected seventeen of his poems for inclusion in *The Oxford Book of Modern Verse* and declared him to be 'one of the great lyric poets of the age'.

Gogarty was educated at Stoneyhurst, Clongowes Wood College and Trinity College, Dublin. On qualifying as a physician his first act was to buy himself a Rolls Royce, an extravagance which his friends questioned but which he explained away. 'I'm going to drive myself into a practice,' he told them.

During the War of Independence and the Civil War period, his house in Ely Place was at the disposal of Michael Collins, to whom Gogarty gave a halldoor key which was returned in tragic circumstances. After the shooting of Collins at Béal na Blath, the bloodstained key was given back to Gogarty: 'A symbol', he commented, 'of Ireland's shame.'

The death of Collins, following so swiftly on that of Arthur Griffith, shocked Gogarty into an abiding abhorrence of the anti-Treaty adherents. 'De Valera's march to cloud cuckoo town,' he said of the Civil War, with a bitterness which his personal experiences went some distance at least in justifying.

In 1923 the houses of thirty-seven Senators of the new State were burned down by the anti-Treaty forces. Gogarty had accepted office as a Senator and Renvyle House was one of them. 'So, Renvyle House' (he wrote) 'with its irreplaceable oaken panelling is burned down. They say it took a week to burn. Blue china fused like solder.'

The destruction of Renvyle House was followed shortly afterwards by an attempt on his own life. Masked gunmen entered Ely Place and took him by car to a deserted house on the banks of the Liffey near Island Bridge and told him to prepare for death. Gogarty delayed matters by pleading, as he himself puts it, 'a natural necessity'. They led him into the garden which bordered the river. It was a dark night in the depths of winter. Gogarty watched for his moment and managed to get away from his escort by slipping out of his loosely fitting overcoat and leaving his two guards holding the empty sleeves. A hail of shots followed his plunge into the icy water but none of them found their target. As he swam for the opposite shore, Gogarty swore to the goddess of the river that if she delivered him safely, he would present her with a pair of swans. Later on, in the company of W.B. Yeats, President W.T. Cosgrave and others, he fulfilled his vow. Today it is said that all the swans on the Liffey are the descendants of Gogarty's gift. He celebrated the event in his volume of poems which he called – appropriately enough – *An Offering of Swans*.

> Keep you these calm and lovely things
> And float them on your clearest water
> For one would not disgrace a King's
> Transformed, beloved and buoyant daughter
> And with her goes this sprightly swan
> A bird of more than royal feather
> With alban beauty clothed upon:
> O keep them fair and well together.

The verse is poised and polished but Gogarty's state of mind in the months after his escape was far from matching it: 'I am only a figment in the imagination of my nation', he wrote, 'and that imagination is not quite sane.'

His answer was to emigrate for a period to England, where once again his reputation as a wit earned him a respected place at political and social occasions. There is a story that, on his return to Ireland, as he was going down the gangway, a sailor touched him on the arm and said: 'Excuse me, Dr Gogarty, but I have a few poems here that I wrote and I was wondering if you'd be good enough to have a look at them.'

'I knew, then,' Gogarty remarked later, 'that I was back in Dublin.'

Gogarty's friendship with Joyce broke down very early in their careers and was never restored. In 1904, when Gogarty rented the Martello tower at Sandycove on Dublin bay he invited Joyce to join him, the idea being that Gogarty should work at his poetry and Joyce at his novel. However, it did not quite work out like that. Gogarty found it impossible to put up with what he regarded as Joyce's rudeness and ingratitude to those who had helped him. 'I have broken with Joyce,' (he wrote) 'his want of generosity became inexcusable . . . a desert was revealed among the seeming luxuriance of his soul.'

Joyce retaliated in *Ulysses* by setting the first scene in the Martello tower and portraying Gogarty in the guise of the first character one meets: Buck Mulligan. In 1937, books were again the source of trouble for Gogarty, this time one of his own. His autobiographical work, *As I was Going Down Sackville Street*, contained some doggerel verses which gave offence to two Dublin antique dealers who subsequently won an action for damages against him. The verdict disgusted Gogarty and the damages seriously depleted his resources. He went to America to lecture and write books which, incidentally, were almost invariably banned in his native country.

In 1957 he returned to Renvyle, his exile ended. He had collapsed in a New York street without anyone knowing who he was. But he had requested that his body should be returned to the west and his wishes were fulfilled. W.T. Cosgrave, Monsignor de Brun, Lennox Robinson, his biographer Ulick O'Connor and several other public figures attended the interment in Ballynakill Churchyard, where today his tombstone carries an epitaph from one of his own poems:

Our friends go with us as we go
Down the long path where Beauty wends,
Where all we love, foregather, so
Why should we fear to join our friends.

Then do not shudder at the knife
That Death's indifferent hand drives home
But with the strivers leave the strife
Nor, after Caesar, skulk in Rome.

(1978)

That Solitary Man

John Millington Synge was born at 2 Newtown Villas, Rathfarnham, near Dublin on 16 April 1871 and died on 24 March 1909, a few weeks short of his thirty-eighth birthday.

Much of his life was spent in a lonely search for two things: a new literary idiom and an answer to what, for him, was unanswerable anyway – the meaning of life and death. It was a search which took him to remote areas of Wicklow, Kerry and Connaught and to the Blaskets and the Aran Islands, where he studied the customs and beliefs of simple people living close to nature, determined, as he once said, 'to put down strong roots among the clay and the worms'.

It was a strange resolve for one of his birth and background. His family was strictly Protestant and totally Ascendancy. Among his ancestors on both sides were several clergymen and no less than five bishops. His mother, herself the daughter of an evangelical rector, sought to fix young Synge's thoughts on the danger of being damned for all eternity, a notion which terrified him on and off until an event which happened around his fourteenth birthday shattered his belief in Christianity and turned him eventually into an agnostic. He took up a book by Darwin one day which opened at a passage where he asks how can the similarity between a man's hand and a bird's or bat's wing be explained except by evolution. The result was (Synge records), 'By the time I was sixteen or seventeen I had renounced Christianity after a good deal of wobbling.'

Unwilling to be hypocritical, he refused after a while to attend religious services, much to the anguish of his mother and the scandal of family and friends. His decision cut him off from any real relationship with his kindred. 'Till I was twenty-three,' he wrote, 'I never met or knew a man or woman who shared my opinions.'

For companionship he turned to those long, solitary journeys in the Dublin and Wicklow mountains which pointed his thoughts towards a new philosophy and provided the material for a new literary style. He also devoted himself to the study of musical composition and the violin, so much so that they claimed him almost exclusively from his sixteenth to his twenty-third year and sent him eventually to Koblenz to pursue his studies. While there, however, he realised that an ungovernable nervousness would always make public performances impossible. Abandoning his musical ambitions, he went to Paris to study languages and literary criticism. It was there Yeats found him in December of 1896 and gave him the, by now, famous advice to give up Paris and to go to Aran to give expression to a culture that had not as yet found an interpreter. Eighteen months later, in the Summer of 1898, Synge made his first of four separate trips to the islands.

There were other reasons besides Yeats' advice which may have drawn him there. An uncle, the Rev Alexander Synge, had ministered for a time on the Aran Islands and, incidentally, had aroused the anger of the islanders by operating a fishing vessel in competition with them. Synge himself had already turned from the loyalist tradition of his family to become a nationalist. Contact with Yeats had roused his sympathy with the ideas of the Literary Revival. The Irish language and Celtic mythology were subjects he had already studied while at Trinity College. There was, in addition, his already noted determination to 'put down strong roots among the clay and the worms'. It is little wonder, then, that on Aran it all came together: an Irish speaking society in a primitive world ordered by nature, where the crafts of survival had to be practised in due season and religious belief found room at once for spirits and fairies and wonders, a faith adjusted instinctively to the savagery of the elements and the cruel toll of the sea. On Aran he found his symbol for the life of the individual: that of a wave, set in motion by natural forces, gathering in size and strength under their influence, and then receding into nothingness again as the original impulses were spent. It was an elemental and uncomplicated concept consistent with his simple and steady grasp of reality.

On Aran, as in Wicklow, West Kerry, Connemara and Mayo, the Gaelic imagery and Gaelic construction grafted on to the English language by the ordinary people first suggested a new and distinctive literary idiom to him. Their stories reflected faithfully those qualities of fantasy, exaggeration and energy he had already encountered in his studies of Celtic mythology. Here was a way of using the English language which had been shaped instinctively by humble peasants to express the needs of their Celtic temperament, in a manner more satisfying than formal English could ever supply. Synge began the work of noting and studying turns of phrase and imagery and speech rhythms. When he was writing *In the Shadow of the Glen* he got more aid than any learning could give (he records) from a chink in the floor which let him hear what the servant girls were saying.

> In countries where the imagination of the people, and the language they use, is rich and living, it is possible for a writer to be rich and copious with words, and at the same time to give the reality, which is the root of all poetry, in a comprehensive and natural form. . . . On the stage one must have reality, and one must have joy, and that is why the intellectual modern drama has failed. . . . In a good play every speech should be as fully flavoured as a nut or apple.

In remote country places he found a popular imagination that was at once fiery, magnificent and tender. Out of it, in a few short years, he shaped six plays for the National Theatre which, as Padraic Colum observed, 'belong essentially to the Gaelic tradition'.

Yet when *In the Shadow of the Glen* was first performed in the Molesworth Hall on 8 October 1903 it aroused fierce nationalist hostility. Its story of the young wife who goes off with a tramp after having been evicted by her ageing husband and abandoned by her young lover was described as a slur on Irish womanhood and a libel on womankind.

The Playboy of the Western World, first produced in January 1907, caused such commotion in the theatre that the police had to be called. The story of a young man being made much of by the girls of Mayo because he had had the mettle to slay his father was too much for patriotic sensibility: 'An unmitigated, protracted libel' (*Freeman's Journal* reported) 'upon Irish peasant men and, worse still, upon Irish peasant girlhood. . . .'

The lead in that first performance was played by a twenty-year-old actress with whom Synge had fallen in love, Molly Allgood, whose stage name was Maire O'Neill. Neither Synge's family nor Yeats nor Lady Gregory approved of the affair. Molly was poor; she had been educated in an orphanage; she had worked as a shopgirl; she was a Catholic. The match seemed altogether unsuitable. But Molly was beautiful and highly gifted as an actress and Synge was determined. Soon she was his constant companion on his walks through County Dublin and Wicklow. At the beginning of 1908, in preparation for their marriage, Synge rented a flat at 47 York Road, Rathmines.

Despite his frequent walking and cycling tours which were often feats of endurance, Synge had been a delicate child and throughout his adulthood had operations on a number of occasions to remove swollen glands which were the symptoms, though he did not know it, of a progressive and incurable condition: Hodgkin's disease. Now he was stricken again and all thoughts of marriage had to be postponed.

Some months later the doctors making further examinations found an inoperable tumour in Synge's side. He knew there was little time left and struggled to complete his last play, *Deirdre of the Sorrows*, which Molly read aloud with him as successive drafts were made. He also collected his verse for publication and corrected his essays on his travels in Ireland. Then, on

24 March 1909, this most reviled of Abbey dramatists died. George Moore recorded Synge's final disappointment:

> Before he died, Synge asked the nurse to wheel his bed into a room where he could see the Wicklow mountains, the hills where he used to go for long, solitary walks, and he was wheeled into the room. But to see them it was necessary to stand up, but Synge could neither stand, nor sit up in his bed. So his last wish remained ungratified, and he died with tears in his eyes.

Yeats, echoing Padraic Colum's judgement, said of the attacks on Synge's works: 'Forms of emotion and thought which the future will recognise as peculiarly Irish, for no other country has the like, are looked upon as un-Irish because of their novelty in a land that is so nearly conquered that it has all but nothing of its own. . . .'

That verdict was accepted ultimately, however slowly. Synge gave the young Abbey Theatre a literature that was unique, universal, yet entirely national.

He is buried in Mount Jerome.

(1979)

I Hear You Calling Me

Sometime in the late 1940s, in a modest house in Terenure, an elderly and much respected musician talked of musical life in Dublin around the turn of the century. It was late in the night and the seldom used sittingroom, smelling just a little of dust, was dimly lit and cluttered with family photographs which anchored it immovably in the age of Victoria. Their subjects were all unflinchingly respectable. Above the mantelpiece framed certificates of early successes with the London College of Music and the Royal Irish Academy proclaimed, in addition, their undoubted musicality.

The usual musical personalities of the age cropped up: Esposito, Vincent O'Brien, T.H. Weaving, Dr Culwick and then, inevitably, J.F. McCormack or, as he preferred to be called later, John McCormack. Mention of the name brought something to the old man's mind and he lifted one of those bulky albums with enormous metal clasps from the table and searched through it, producing at last a yellowed piece of paper which turned out to be a programme for a concert which had been held in the Antient Concert Rooms in Dublin away back in August of 1904. His sister, also a musician, had conducted the orchestra. But more interesting still were two names that succeeded one another among the list of performers:

Mr James A. Joyce
Mr J.F. McCormack

It is an item which has been much reproduced since but

that night it was a new sight, and extremely moving, a fugitive witness to a society that long ago packed its bags and took its leave. It was a society that lingers on only in the work of its artists: in the writings of James Joyce and, in a way that uniquely belongs to music, in the songs of John McCormack.

John McCormack was recognised as a singer of exceptional ability from his earliest years, so much so that he was assisted from the beginning by admiring friends and well-wishers, who knew he was poor enough in those days to need all the help that could be got. He was born in Athlone on 14 June 1884, the fourth child in a family of eleven, whose father worked as a foreman in the local woollen mills which stood on the banks of the Shannon. The rent of their house was a modest three shillings or so a week and his father's earnings would have left no hope whatever of any special schooling or training.

However, the boy made the most of the schooling he got from the Marist Brothers in Athlone and then, in 1896, when he was twelve years old, he won a scholarship to Summerhill College in Athlone. Two subsequent scholarships supported him until it was time to leave. He was eighteen years old, bright and intelligent, with a particular gift for mathematics and languages, an intense love of music and a voice that was recognised on all sides as exceptional. But the voice was untrained and he had no access to technical knowledge of music.

The first to help him with the rudiments of technique was the organist in St Peter's Church in Athlone, a little man by the name of Michael Kilkelly, a grocer by trade who once upon a time had had his own dreams which, however, he had lacked sufficient executant talent to realise. He took the young John into the choir of St Peter's, lavished attention on him and badgered his father to do something to have the lad trained. The father was unable to respond. There was simply no money. So Michael Kilkelly and some young friends wrote to Vincent O'Brien, the conductor of the Pro-Cathedral Choir in Dublin and leading Irish authority on vocal training.

O'Brien was impressed and responded by taking John into the choir at a salary of £25 per year. With this and the help

of a small number of functions and engagements, McCormack
survived. He was not yet nineteen years of age, but he was
in the hands of the best teacher Dublin could provide. A year
later, after intensive tuition, he not only won the gold medal
for tenor in the Feis Ceoil competition of 1903, but did it in
so outstanding a fashion as to cause considerable excitement
in Dublin musical circles. In the competition of the following
year, the young James Joyce (he was 22) forfeited the gold
medal because he refused the sight test – on artistic grounds,
according to himself – but more likely simply because he
could not sight read.

They were exciting times for Dublin and for young artists:
the Gaelic revival movement was in its most enthusiastic and
scholarly phase, the Literary Revival was well under way;
W.B. Yeats, George Moore, J.M. Synge, Lady Gregory, and
the eccentric Edward Martyn (who had endowed the Palestrina
Choir of the Pro-Cathedral out of his great wealth as a
landowner in Galway) were writing plays and weathering the
interminable controversies that dog the Irish literary and
artistic world. On 16 June of 1904 James Joyce met and was
accepted by Nora Barnacle and the first Bloomsday was born.
A short while before, John McCormack had met his own
lifelong partner and companion, Lily Foley.

It was a cold Christmas morning and Lily and her sister
Molly were on their way to sing in the choir at the six o'clock
Mass in Clarendon Street, when a young man in a frieze coat
with an unconvincing looking fur collar passed them. Molly
plucked her sister Lily's arm and said: 'Do you know who
that was? It's young McCormack and he's going to the Pro-
Cathedral to sing at the six o'clock Mass.'

Lily turned around and caught him doing the same. 'I could
feel my cheeks burn,' she reports in her autobiography. But
later they laughed together about it and within a couple of
years they were married. He was twenty-two, Lily was not quite
twenty. That was in July 1906.

The honeymoon in London included as many visits to the
Opera as could be fitted in; more, Lily felt, than they could

afford. They fell out briefly over John's extravagance and disregard for money, even when the source of further supplies was quite uncertain. It was a characteristic which stayed with him all his life, but one he could indulge more freely as success came his way.

Before the marriage Vincent O'Brien had sent John for lessons in Italy, through the help of friends and admirers who arranged a series of concerts to raise the money to pay for the venture. Now, with the money supply petering out, he and Lily decided to go back there in the hope of finding engagements in the Opera. But such work as he found was insufficient to provide a livelihood and they returned to London together to live in poverty, a condition which is no more than the commonplace lot of most aspiring young operatic tenors. He borrowed petty sums to keep himself and Lily going and was helped in small ways by friends and through some recording engagements put in his way by the few agents he had so far managed to impress. Early in 1907 Lily, who was expecting her first child, had to return to her mother in Dublin while John stayed on in London and continued to take whatever work cropped up. In the spring of 1907 their son, Cyril, was born and work became even more urgently necessary.

Success came later in the same year with McCormack's debut at Covent Garden as Turiddu in *Cavalleria Rusticana* on 15 October. The audience shouted his name again and again at the fall of the curtain and the next morning the critics reported their full approval. But he had had another success earlier which was to be of even greater importance in shaping his career than the operatic stage.

The death of a young and beautiful girl of tuberculosis so devastated her fiancé that he was moved to write about it. The bereaved lover used the pen name Harold Harford and the name of the lyric was 'I Hear You Calling Me.' The music publishers refused to touch it but it came into the possession of an accompanist, Charles Marshall, who worked with McCormack. He composed music for it and showed the result to McCormack, who was enthusiastic and sang it at his

next ballad concert. It was a resounding success. McCormack
wrote later:

> One song more than any other has been identified with
> my career and my success all over the world. I have sung
> it in London, Dublin, Berlin and Prague and in far-off
> Australia, New Zealand, Japan, China, South Africa and
> all over the United States, Canada and Hawaii. That song
> is 'I Hear You Calling Me'.

In fact, the tug-o-war between operatic performances and the
art of the drawingroom ballad became central to McCormack's
musical career until at last he made the conscious decision
to abandon opera and to concentrate solely on being a concert
artist.

In doing so he was to become loved everywhere, but
especially in his native Ireland, as a unique tenor. In the
opinion of many he was the greatest of all time. Certainly his
concerts packed out and his records sold universally: at one
stage it was reckoned that he was earning the equivalent of
two million pounds a year in royalties.

John McCormack knew how to work, driving himself and
his accompanists for hours on end while he sought perfection
of phrasing and articulation. But he also knew how to enjoy
life. Before a concert he would take nothing all day except the
lightest of snacks. After the recital he had his friends to his
home for music, merriment and champagne suppers. He was
regarded as warmly for his good fellowship as he was for his
unique gifts by the celebrities of his age. His singing ensured
for his native country her place in the international world
of music.

John McCormack died in Booterstown, Dublin, on Sunday
16 September 1945. He was sixty-one years of age.

(1984)

3

The Mission of Discontent

When Jim Larkin came to Dublin in 1908 he was thirty-two years of age – a handsome young man, tall and broad-shouldered, with a commanding presence. His hat was dark and wide-brimmed – and my mother remembers it being rumoured in those early days that he never removed it because he was anti-Christ and was obliged to hide a third eye that was set in the centre of his forehead.

Indeed, many terrible things had been said about him already. During the Belfast labour troubles of the previous year, for instance, the press, having warned its readers on different occasions that he was either a socialist, an anarchist, or a syndicalist, decided to make the case against him as black as possible by labelling him a papist. Very soon the press in Dublin, with a similar desire to suit its revelations to its audience, was referring to him as an orangeman. Later it decided he was an atheist. When this failed to dislodge him from the esteem of his devoted 'rabble of carters and dockers', a photograph of Larkin appeared in one newspaper side by side with a drawing of Carey, the informer. In the caption above the photographs the question was put to the readers: 'Is Larkin the son of Carey?' So it will be seen right away that, had Larkin been so endowed, a third eye would have been a comparatively minor handicap.

As it happened, Jim Larkin, born in 1876, was the second son of impoverished Irish parents who had emigrated to

Liverpool, and he had spent nearly all of the first five years of his childhood with his grandparents in Newry. It was a very brief childhood. At the age of nine he was back in Liverpool, a breadwinner now, working forty hours a week for a wage of two shillings and sixpence – plus a penny bun and a glass of milk which his employer gave him every weekend as a sort of bonus. Later, he went to sea and sailed to South America; then, on his return to Liverpool, he became a foreman on the docks, until he lost his job through coming out in sympathy with the men under him. This action of his – the first blow in a fight which was to last his lifetime – led to a position as temporary organiser for the National Union of Dockers.

The appointment proved very temporary indeed. Jim Larkin's militant methods during the Belfast disputes of 1907 alarmed not only the employers, but the executive of the union he served. James Sexton, the general secretary, said of him:

> Jim Larkin crashed upon the public with the devastating roar of a volcano exploding without even a preliminary wisp of smoke. I have myself been called an agitator and have not resented it. Believe me, however, in my earliest and hottest days of agitating I was more frigid than a frozen millpond in comparison with Larkin. . . . I was feeble, tongue-tied, almost dumb.

And, what was worse in James Sexton's eyes, Larkin proved himself quite unamenable to discipline. In Belfast his new weapons of the sympathetic strike, his doctrine of tainted goods and his wildfire oratory closed down job after job with alarming inevitability. He persuaded the members of the police force who were supposed to be keeping the strikers in order that they were underpaid for this difficult and unpopular work – and it ended with the police going on strike too. Belfast became an armed camp, with soldiers bivouacking in the streets. All this was far too fast and furious for the Liverpool executive. Alarmed at the turn events had taken, they took matters out of his hands altogether by excluding him from the negotiations and the ultimate settlement.

Larkin was not a man, either then or at any point throughout a stormy lifetime, to submit to being overruled by others. Besides, the conservative outlook of the accepted trade unionism of the time did not appeal to him. Already he had plans in mind for the formation of an Irish-based union which would make full use of the new revolutionary techniques under his own control and leadership. And already, in the imaginations of the more timorous, he was the Visitation With The Third Eye.

Dublin, in 1908, provided as disturbing a picture as any revolutionary might look on. In order to see the events of those early years in proper perspective, let us spend a little time examining that society, through some official records that have been left for us. At that time the population of the city, which then excluded Pembroke, Rathmines and Rathgar, was 305,000 people, of whom 87,000 (or about one third) lived under quite terrible conditions. These destitute 87,000 people occupied the cast-off houses of the rich and they walked about – for the most part – in the cast-off clothes of the middle classes. D.A. Chart in a lecture delivered about this time, gives us a picture of children and old people searching the bins of the well-to-do for cinders; so that even the fuel of the poor, or a substantial part of it, was gathered through the same casting-off process.

The tenement houses were divided by the housing inquiry of 1913, in its official report, into three categories:

> Those which appeared structurally sound; those so decayed as to be on the borderline of being unfit for human habitation and those unfit for human habitation and incapable of being rendered fit for human habitation.

The structurally sound houses accommodated 27,000 persons; the borderline houses 37,500; while 23,000 people lived in the tenements which the commission had declared to be absolutely unfit for habitation. In other words, one third of the population lived under conditions injurious to physique and morality.

So much for the houses. Now let us look at the living

conditions by examining some typical evidence given at the
enquiry. One witness described seeing a room sixteen feet
square occupied by the two parents and their seven children.
They slept on the floor, on which, according to the witness,
there was not enough straw to accommodate a cat and no
covering of any kind whatever. The children were poorly clad;
one wrapped in a rag of a kind, and his only other clothing
a very dirty loin cloth. Furniture? Nothing. A zinc bucket, a
can, a few mugs or jampots for drinking. Rent – two shillings
and threepence weekly; wages – over some weeks four shillings
and sixpence a week, with a maximum in a considerable period
of twelve shillings.

Similar pictures were painted by other witnesses, but there
is no need to repeat them; the opposition ended by admitting
the facts. In doing so, they showed another aspect of the Dublin
situation which must be considered in any study of Jim Larkin
and his message. It demonstrates, I think, that his task was
to bring about a revolutionary change in social attitudes. He
himself, in his characteristic evangelical style, announced that
he had come – I quote his phrase – 'to preach the divine
mission of discontent'. That mission, in fact, was to create a
new social conscience.

The social thinking of the period is typified in a book
published in 1914. It was written by Arnold Wright at the
request of the Dublin Chamber of Commerce to explain to
the world the employers' side of the 1913 struggle, so it is
reasonable to accept it as expressing their outlook. In it Mr
Wright deals with the findings of the housing inquiry and
admits quite freely that living conditions were appalling:

> While it is impossible to withhold sympathy from classes
> so depressed as these slum dwellers of Dublin are, it
> cannot be overlooked that the very nature of their mode
> of living tends to reduce their value in the labour market.
> One point upon which witness after witness insisted
> (during the course of giving evidence at the housing
> inquiry) was the physical deterioration of men who find

their way into these terrible hovels. Once drawn into the abyss they speedily lose, not merely their sense of self-respect, but their capacity for sustained exertion. At the same time the thought of all that is implied in this vicious housing system in the way of demoralisation and decadence of physical powers, should make us chary of playing the role of critic to employers who have to use this damaged material.

While Mr Wright was blaming the housing conditions as the cause of physical deterioration, the landlords were equally bitter. Their complaint was that they could not make a business proposition of letting their houses unless they crammed the tenants in in large numbers, because in smaller numbers per house the tenants were unable to afford an economic rent. This was a heads-I-win, harps-you-lose situation. In the eyes of the landlords, these slum dwellers were rent-paying units to be crammed into every available inch of space. They saw the economic problem, but failed to suspect that there was also a moral one. To Mr Wright and the employers on whose behalf he wrote, the slum dweller, working sixty hours a week for an average wage of sixteen shillings had lost his value in the labour market because (in Mr Wright's words) his capacity for sustained exertion was impaired by his living conditions. He was 'damaged material' – not a unique creature made in God's image. That the 87,000 slum dwellers who were enduring all this had any rights to consideration as human beings does not seem to have occurred to anybody. James Joyce spoke of Dublin as the centre of paralysis. It was a total paralysis, blinding conscience and soul. It remained to Jim Larkin to see the slum dweller as a human being: degraded, yet capable of nobility, perceptive, capable of living with dignity, capable, even, of music and literature. That was the message he began to address to the city at large – a message of love, delivered, one must concede, by a man swinging wildly about him with a sword.

The Irish Transport & General Workers' Union, which he

formed in 1909, was designed to cater for the masses of unskilled workers – carters, dockers, labourers, factory-hands and so on – for whom there had been no effective organisation before his arrival. While the militancy of this new body was startling Dublin out of its moral and intellectual paralysis, Larkin made effective appeals to the skilled workers and the craft unions to help the unskilled men in their fight and to abandon the customary snobbery that distinguished between the bowler hat and the cloth cap. Meanwhile, because drink played its part in the degradation of the poor, he launched a private temperance campaign and succeeded, at least to the extent of having the custom of making wages offices out of certain public houses abolished. Corruption and jobbery he attacked by frontal methods that were typical of his style – naming the offenders and prodding at them in speech after speech until he created uproar; and sometimes, let it be confessed, naming the wrong people in his enthusiasm. He thundered against low wages and bad housing in nightly harangues that mixed the vernacular with quotations from Whitman and Shelley. The masses listened spellbound, even when they didn't quite understand. James Connolly returned from America in 1910 to find the industrial world torn by strikes and lock-outs. In those furious onslaughts of Dublin's lowliest toilers he saw his watchword 'What we want is less philosophizing and more fighting' in daily operation. Soon Connolly was in the struggle too as an official of the union.

From 1908 to 1913 the business life of the city staggered from crisis to crisis, the unskilled workers in revolt, the employers fighting back, at first individually, then with attempted solidarity through their federation, which was formed in 1911. At this stage the development of simple machinery for direct negotiation might have eased the situation. Instead, however, the archaic pattern continued; the union served its demands, the employers rejected them, the men went on strike. When Larkin suggested that the employers should meet the workers' representatives for direct negotiations, it was looked on, for the most part, as further evidence of his vanity and his arrogance. The solution eventually proposed to the federation was the banning of the union altogether. This led to a head-on clash and the tragic struggle of 1913.

The battle opened in August of that year, when employees throughout the city were issued with a form and requested to sign. The document contained this sentence: 'I agree to immediately resign my membership of the Irish Transport & General Workers' Union (if a member) and I further undertake that I will not join or in any way support that union.' The document was issued indiscriminately to Transport Union members and members of various other unions.

The decision to issue it may have been based on a miscalculation, on the assumption that Larkinism could be isolated from the rest of trade unionism and liquidated separately. For some months many employers had been carrying extra staff, with the intention of using these men to replace Transport Union men if a lock-out became necessary. William Martin Murphy, the employers' spokesman, stated publicly that 'he had no apprehension that a strike would be attempted, and no fear at all – if it was attempted – that it would last a single day'.

Despite what Mr Murphy had to say, the Transport men refused to sign the document and, as the time limit in each job expired, they were locked out. The machinery of intimidation then went into action. Police reinforcements were drafted into the city, police pensioners were called back and sworn in to do duty as gaolers, the military were alerted and stood by in readiness. Larkinism and Society stood face to face, ready for battle.

It was at this point that Larkin's grip on the Dublin working class was revealed at its most impressive. He had proved his extraordinary power in Belfast in 1907 when he persuaded nationalist and orange workers to march together as an expression of class solidarity. He proved it again in Dublin in August 1913, when the members of thirty-two other unions in the city took their stand firmly on the side of the Larkinites and refused to sign the employers' document. This colossal expression of defiance shocked the federation. Four hundred firms began to lock out right, left and centre. Soon the city was paralysed and about 100,000 people faced hunger and want. They faced it for eight months. And, by and large, remained stubborn to the end.

Jim Larkin's great task, as I have said, was to create a new social conscience. His efforts, of course, were only one part of a broader struggle which was being fought the world over: in Russia through the Bolshevists, in America through the IWW, along the Clyde and in Liverpool and other industrial centres where liberal England was in its death throes and the great fight between socialism and toryism was being joined. Larkin fought spectacularly. When funds ran low he rallied enormous support from the British working class as a result of a campaign in Britain. He called it, dramatically, 'The Fiery Cross Campaign'. He brought ships steaming up the Liffey with food for his locked-out followers – another dramatic gesture. It would have been easier to send the money, of course, but Larkin always chose the extravagant and the heroic. He knew that to hold 100,000 hungry people together you needed something more dramatic than a subscription list. Ships steaming in with flags, torchlight processions and bands, songs and slogans and the thunder of speeches from the windows of Liberty Hall, these were his weapons, and he calculated that a man with an empty belly would stand the pain of it better if you could succeed in filling his head full of poetry. Those who previously had nothing with which to fill out the commonplace of drab days could now march in processions, wave torches, yell out songs and cheer their own ships as they bore down the Liffey with food and good tidings. Men cannot live on poetry forever. But it is an ennobling experience to live on it for even a little while. It was Larkin's triumph to inject enough of it into a starving class to lift them off their knees and lead them out of the pit.

His methods attracted the best spirits in Ireland to the workers' side, and as a result of 1913 the cause of the poor became identified with their larger plans for a new and free Ireland. Padraic Pearse wrote in support of the workers and showed his sympathy with Larkin in a practical way by keeping his two sons at St Enda's. Yeats, AE, Bernard Shaw, Tom Kettle, Joseph Plunkett, Thomas MacDonagh, Eamon Ceannt, James Stephens and Padraic Colum came in on Larkin's side. Countess Markiewicz and Mrs Sheehy Skeffington laboured in the soup kitchens of Liberty Hall and helped to feed the hungry wives and children of the strikers. There were, of course, those who disapproved. Arthur Griffith attacked Larkin bitterly in *Sinn Fein* and spoke of 'the vile and destructive methods of demagogues posing as strike leaders'. Larkin's attempt to send children of the strikers to English homes was publicly denounced. His plan to remove them for a little while from a city of hunger and want was regarded as a danger to their faith and morals. Clergy and laity patrolled the railway stations and the quaysides and snatched the children away from those who were in charge of them. Sometimes, in their zeal, they snatched the wrong children and left perfectly respectable fathers and mothers arguing desperately for the return of their offspring. Frank Sheehy Skeffington was an active helper in the effort to get the children to England; Sir William Orpen, who used to visit Larkin's office in Liberty Hall, has left a picture of Skeffington back from one of these engagements wrapped in a blanket for decency's sake – his clothes had been torn off him. But perhaps Larkin himself put this sorry interlude in proper perspective. 'It's a poor religion,' he said, 'that won't stand up to a fortnight's holidays.'

When the struggle ended, the right of a hitherto forgotten class to consideration in any plan for a free Ireland had been planted firmly in the minds of the nation's leaders. In addition, the Citizen Army existed, pledged to the cause of a workers' republic. 'God Save Ireland' was the slogan of the middle-class nationalist who dreamed of restoring to Kathleen Ni Hoolihaun her four green fields. 'God Save The People' answered the leaders of the Citizen Army, who, to paraphrase James Connolly, were not prepared to destroy British capitalism simply for the sake of replacing it by Irish capitalism. They had more revolutionary plans than that, which they hoped to realise through the Irish Citizen Army, formed during the 1913 strike and reconstituted in 1914, with Larkin as its first commandant, to fight for the establishment of a workers' republic. Later Connolly's influence brought both nationalists and Citizen Army men together in a closer understanding and in 1916 they fought side by side.

By this time, however, Larkin had gone to America, to raise funds, as he announced, to rebuild the union and to tell American labour of Irish problems and methods. While there he barely escaped hanging at the hands of hired thugs on a couple of occasions, and eventually he was sentenced to ten years' penal servitude for what the court termed 'Criminal Syndicalism'. He served three years in Sing Sing before being released by order of Governor Al Smith in 1923.

For the first time since 1914 Larkin found himself with permission and means of returning to Ireland. His journey was a progress of triumph. American workers lined the docks to cheer him off; at Southampton the British workers turned up in their thousands to pay him honour. In Dublin the streets from Westland Row station to Liberty Hall were packed with people; young men unyoked the wagonette in which he was travelling and themselves dragged it through the streets. Five bands marched in the procession and the people sang strike songs and shouted the slogans of 1913.

This high moment of triumph was the prelude to a bitter split. The union had grown enormously strong during his absence. Its part in the 1913 struggle, the fame of Larkin's exploits, Connolly's execution in 1916, its association with 1916 through many of its officials and members and through the Irish Citizen Army, all these things endeared it to the ordinary people. But to Larkin's mind things were not well. He had planned to return with a food ship for the relief of dependants of political prisoners, as a prelude to a campaign for unity and an end to fratricidal strife. The executive of the union had refused. He had not forgotten the hostility of Arthur Griffith and distrusted the outlook of his successors in power. The policy of wage cuts which the government was pursuing seemed to him to be proof enough that labour's share in the philosophy of the new state was being gobbled up by the nationalists. In fact he had expressed this fear in letters from America after the rising. 'The gang here,' he wrote (meaning the Irish Americans) 'are more fearful of *our* movement getting ahead in Eire than if Johnny Bull played the same game as in '98. They make out Arthur G. as a Godgiven saint and statesman. Nobody in Ireland did anything but Sinn Fein. Connolly and the other boys all recanted socialism and labour and were good Sinn Feiners. My God, it is sickening.' Larkin felt the the union was not acting forcefully enough to put the case of labour and socialism to the Irish people. His view was the same as that expressed in 1919 by Sean O'Casey when he predicted in his *Story of the Citizen Army* that 'Labour would probably have to fight Sinn Fein'.

Although Larkin was still general secretary, there were members on the executive committee who were antagonistic to him. Besides, he was never a man to allow an executive to overrule him. He provoked a legal battle for control of the union, declaring the executive to be illegally elected. He lost and was expelled from the union he had formed fourteen years before. Within a few months of his triumphal return Larkin, an undischarged bankrupt, was expelled by his colleagues and hated by the government. The last prophet of the workers' republic was a national outcast. But a penniless Larkin had assets no law or committee could strip him of. They were courage, a magnetic personality, and a superb gift of oratory. Within months he had rallied his old guard of carters and dockers, founded another union, and was leading strikes with undefeated vigour and recklessness. Gradually he assumed leadership once more in the eclipsed world of gaslight and tenement and gradually he won his way into public life. Pearse was dead and Connolly was dead and Skeffington, and all the other great hearts who had room for his passionate views of an Ireland of the people. He fought his way alone, re-establishing his influence through the Dublin Trades Council and the activities of his new union – the Workers' Union of

Ireland. He became a city councillor and on two occasions
a deputy of Dail Éireann. In the nineteen-forties he led a
campaign against the Wages Standstill Order and succeeded
in forcing amending legislation. His last large-scale efforts were
to help in the foundation of a union for agricultural workers
and the formulation of a demand for a fortnight's annual leave
for manual workers, which after a fourteen weeks' strike was
generally conceded.

In the course of forty years of social agitation Jim Larkin
earned a reputation which was universal. Yet he was no
doctrinaire revolutionary in the Continental sense and he was
no great theorist. R.M. Fox, in his biography, speaks of him
as a socialist of the old British school, a description which is
near enough to the mark, but still inadequate. Perhaps the
employers of Dublin found the best name for his movement
when they labelled it Larkinism. His lifelong concern was
not with theory, but with the immediate needs of the underprivileged – the sweated men, the struggling mothers, the
little children born to a life of drudgery in a sunless world.
In his efforts to help them he was sometimes arrogant,
sometimes unfair to colleagues and often rash beyond the
justification of his most indulgent admirers. He could fling
a terrible phrase at the employers – 'You'll crucify Christ no
longer in this town' – and then turn with equal venom on
his religious critics. Once, when an eminent churchman
warned the people against him he said:

> Hell has no terrors for me. I've lived there. Thirty-six
> years of hunger and poverty have been my portion. The
> mother who bore me had to starve and work, and the
> father I loved had to fight for a living. I knew what it
> was to work when I was nine years old. They can't terrify
> me with hell. Better to be in hell with Dante and Davitt
> than to be in heaven with Carson and Murphy.

This, no doubt, is emotive argument, but it makes a point
that is larger than the measure of its logic. Larkin was adept
at returning bombs before they had time to explode.

For the rest, he was a man of sober habits and few wants and he walked throughout life, as he himself said, 'always in the fear of God, but never in the fear of any man'. When he died in 1947, he left behind him some personal articles, a little furniture and four pounds and ten shillings in money, the balance of his weekly wages.

1946 had seen the setting up of the Labour Court, which symbolised the victory of trade unionism in its fight for a respected and influential place in the social and economic life of modern Ireland. Here was the beginning of a new stage in labour relations, with its machinery for direct negotiation and conciliation, representing new privileges for trade unionism, but also placing on its shoulders new responsibilities. Jim Larkin was the last of the great militants, and with his funeral on that bleak day in February of 1947, when thousands stood in the slush and the cold to bid him farewell, an era of titanic struggle moved peacefully to an end.

(1961)

Changed Times

In February 1947, as one of thousands of others, I marched in the funeral of Big Jim Larkin. There had been a blizzard the day before and snow lay thickly in the streets. All the shops were closed, the flags along the route were at half-mast, traffic was at a standstill. It was an occasion that has the power to move even in retrospect. And looking back at it now, I know we were laying to rest, on that bitterly cold morning, not only a great man, but a whole era.

Larkin was the last of the great revolutionaries. Forty or so years before he had come to Ireland to preach – I use his own much-quoted phrase – the 'divine mission of discontent', and he had found there, and particularly in Dublin, as harrowing a picture as any revolutionary might look on. The population of the city was then around 305,000 people; 87,000 of them (about one third) lived under quite terrible conditions, in tenements which were condemned by an official commission of the time as being in most cases totally unfit for human habitation. Large families were crowded into single rooms; often a solitary lavatory in a back yard was expected to serve the needs of anything from seventy to ninety people. The death rate was alarming. In 1900, for instance, it was forty-six per thousand as against eighteen or nineteen in English cities.

Working conditions were equally appalling. Half the population of the city, almost 170,000, were classified as being in the unskilled or casual and unproductive categories. The average wage for men was fourteen shillings for a week of seventy hours; women would work for even longer periods for anything from five to ten shillings a week. Society as a whole either ignored or overlooked the plight of this submerged third of the city's population, while the employers were quite genuinely convinced that labour was a commodity to be bought with the lowest wage possible and that in giving employment they acquired automatically the right to regulate every moment of an employee's working week.

Trade Union organisation among the unskilled and casual workers was negligible. There were the Craft Unions, of course, with established rights in the regulation of pay and working conditions which had a long and respected history in the city. But the skilled men shared with the middle and upper classes the view that the tenement dwellers were a breed apart, to be avoided and, often enough, despised. At the beginning of his campaign Larkin had three main tasks to accomplish: First, to implant in the unskilled and casual workers a confidence in their own ability to confront exploitation, and a pride in the humble but necessary roles they played in the community. Second, he had to win for them the right to be heard on issues affecting working conditions, wages and living standards. Third, he had to bring Irish society generally to an awareness of the injustice, suffering and deprivation in its cellars (so to speak) and by doing so to create a new social conscience.

These tasks he accomplished to greater or lesser extents in a series of battles which he waged between 1907 in Belfast and 1913 in Dublin, the bitterest, but also, in the long run, the most fruitful in winning sympathy and influential support. By the time the eight-month-long lock-out came to its inconclusive end, the city was in no doubt about the appalling conditions of its poorest citizens and the need for social reform, however minimal. As to the right of the unskilled to have a voice in rates of pay and working conditions, however practice may have lagged behind, the principle at least was acknowledged in paragraph 18 of the Report of the Government Inquiry into the Lock-Out. It reads:

All the great industries of every civilized country have long recognised that trade and manufacture can only be conducted by the practical acceptance on the part of both employers and employed of the fact that there is a mutual interest, and that such interest can only be adjusted satisfactorily by friendly discussion. Irish employers and Irish workers will find they can be no exception to this modern development.

The Inquiry then goes on to propose methods of conciliation.

That, then, was about as far as general trade unionism in Ireland had progressed up to the outbreak of the First World War. It had established its right to organise; it had forced a number of inquiries into such matters as work procedures, rates of pay, and housing conditions; it had won official endorsement for the view that the employee had a right to be heard.

But perhaps the most important legacy from the lock-out was the place it itself was to attain in Irish working-class mythology. 1913, the Citizen Army, the food ships, the kitchens in Liberty Hall feeding the multitude, the monster meetings and the torchlight processions, these glowed inwardly in later years among the outward bleakness. In addition to such hard won assets, acquired through a dogged – one might say, intractable – heroism, and sense of fellowship, the general trade union movement brought with it into the new dispensation of the Irish Free State a powerful rallying slogan – 'An injury to one is the concern of all' – and three proven weapons: Larkin's doctrine of 'tainted goods' ('tainted', that is, through the intervention of the strike-breaker in their manufacture or distribution); the use of the sympathetic strike; and an almost unreasoning reverence for the picket, that left it wide open to sectional exploitation and abuse.

As it turned out in that period between the two wars, Irish trade unionism needed every resource it could tap in a new Free State that had formidable problems. The aftermath of the Civil War had implanted bitter, personal hatreds which absorbed much of the energies of the leaders. Partition and the oath of allegiance enmeshed the country in difficult, nationalistic abstractions. The Bolshevik revolution had spread such terror among Irish secular and ecclesiastical establishments that orthodoxy, suspicious of everything, including convictions of almost any liberal kind, reinforced the stoutly capitalist outlook of the new State. By 1932, a total of twelve or more organisations had been suppressed after an all-out drive against left-wing influences. In these circumstances, the outlook for trade unionism, particularly for that among the unskilled and the lowly, was not encouraging.

The economic practicalities were even more dismal. A policy of wage cuts, both here and in England, absorbed the movement in negative and wholly defensive struggles; on the docks and in the railways and the building industry in 1924; in the coal trade in 1926; and in another railways dispute over wage cuts and redundancies in 1929. In the beginning of all this, 40,000 demobbed men from the national army were thrown on the labour market, either without any regard, or with a very studied regard, to the effect on the availability of work. Meanwhile, in the world outside, the United States had its Wall Street Crash followed by a huge unemployment problem, and in Britain the hunger marchers were mustering.

To make matters worse, a great split developed in the movement as a result of hostility between William O'Brien and Jim Larkin, a split which divided trade unionism in one way or another from 1923 to the end of the fifties. The effect of these difficulties was a falling-off in membership: the ITUC had an affiliated membership of almost 200,000 in 1922; by 1929 the figure had dropped to under 100,000.

But, if viewed from the present, the Irish scene from the founding of the State to the end of the Second World War wears a grey and depressing air, it is not simply because of the economic circumstances, bad as they were. It is not so much the poverty, the insecurity, the indignities and heartbreak that attend any situation of under-employment, for these were the common burden of most of the world throughout the hungry thirties. It is not even the deplorable waste of time and spirit that attended the interminable barney between Treatyite and anti-Treatyite with its besetting displays of flag-waggery. There is much more than that. There is that type of arid and instant scholasticism, peculiarly Irish and particularly rampant, in that period which addressed itself to each and every social debate, solely, it appeared, to show why nothing must be changed. There were strong authoritarian assumptions in Church and State, which took advantage of the average citizen's – and therefore of the ordinary trade unionist's – religious and national loyalties, in a period when the outstanding marks of plain Joe Soap were a sincere if befuddled patriotism and an ingenuous acceptance of authority.

Coming up to the Second World War Joe Soap was earning (if he had work, that is) around two pounds, ten shillings to three pounds a week, figures that have little meaning nowadays, so let us put it another way: in 1938 his average income was 49% of that of his opposite number in Britain (it had been better back in 1931 – 61%). He worked five and a half days a week, probably forty-four to forty-eight hours. The Holidays for Employees Act entitled him to one week's paid leave in the year, which only gave him a legal right to something he had won for himself already. If married, he usually spent that week of leisure at home. If young and single, he might venture as far as Liverpool or the Isle of Man. Continental travel was undreamt of.

In marriage, his role and that of his wife's were fixed and unambiguous: he the wage-earner, the breadwinner, she the home-maker and manager of the domestic budget. The idea that she too might go out to work hardly entered anyone's head. Both of them expected the children to contribute to the household economy when they themselves began to earn and, generally speaking, they did, for that was the general practice.

In politics, Joe Soap was more likely to vote Fianna Fail than Labour, because his attention was still easily captured by the Treaty versus the anti-Treaty arguments. He saw politics and social reform as separate issues – if indeed he regarded social reform as a practical issue at all. In the world of work, generally speaking, he distrusted his employer. Whenever he could get away with it, he limited his output, not because he was lazy or basically dishonest, but because if the same volume of production was done by fewer men, then it was highly likely that he himself or some of his mates would end up on the breadline. His attitude to trade union negotiation procedures was uncomplicated: serve the demand and, when it was refused, serve strike notice.

After that the talking could start. In the case of a wage demand, his usual tactic was to ask for twice as much as he reckoned he might be able to get. I remember Jim Larkin (young Jim) being instructed to serve a demand for a wage increase of X shillings a week and asking the meeting if someone would outline for him the *case* for an increase of X shillings. And I remember the simple answer that won a lot of supporting applause: 'You make the case, Jim, we'll do the fighting'.

In those days, nevertheless, Joe Soap submitted quietly enough to the idea of certain disciplines. The Boss was the Boss; you did what you were told. For misbehaviour on the job he expected to get his cards and usually did. Misbehaviour could be cheeking the foreman or striking a colleague or having drink taken or even smoking.

As I said earlier, the period under review wears a grey and depressing air. The outbreak of the Second World War, in addition to the usual shortages and restrictions, brought with it an Emergency Powers Order declaring a standstill on wages, an order only ameliorated nominally by the subsequent Emergency Powers Bonus Order. Nevertheless, although they appeared so stagnant and isolated, during those years of the war something had been moving all the time in the reflective deeps of the collective mind. Perhaps it was that self-sufficiency had become a condition of survival and that in the government's consultations with industry and trade union interests, which were a vital necessity, attitudes had to be revised. Whatever it was, it seems that during those years of isolation and mutual dependence in Ireland trade unionism had been acquiring a tardy respectability; the notion had been forming, however hazily, that the movement might have a reasonable claim to participation and a contribution to make in the post-war national debate.

Indicative of that new thinking was the setting up of the Labour Court in 1946. Its immediate purpose was to impose some consistency in the handling of the flood of wage claims which would come with the removal of the Wages Standstill Order after almost five years of operation. But the Court's more enduring effect was to confirm the status of the trade union movement in post-war Ireland and, at the same time, to impose on it new responsibilities. The formal nature of the Court's hearings and the fact that it required written submissions set a new style and introduced more exacting negotiation procedures. New techniques of presentation were required – on both sides, let it be said – in which facts and figures acquired new relevance and importance. To the negotiator this meant – to put it squarely – more mind and less mouth.

Trade unionism began to address itself to a continuous analytical scrutiny of the economic and social scene. The need for facts and for expertise in their interpretation led Congress to set up a Department of Research where statistics and other relevant information were collected and circulated to serve the negotiating needs of all affiliated bodies. The first national wage agreement in 1948 also helped to establish procedures that were to become almost standardised. Meanwhile, a new self-consciousness was developing throughout the movement – though not everywhere and all at once. But procedures for annual delegate conferences began to be streamlined and the meeting rooms of general executive committees took on an air of serious business and even of modest comfort, though in some cases it hardly went beyond the disappearance of the solitary electric light bulb that used to hang in naked isolation beneath the plaster cracks on the ceiling.

Then, in the mid-fifties, began the great influx of white-collar workers, whose allegiance had shifted at last away from its long established alliance with management and away from its once entrenched notion that trade unions were less than respectable. This erosion of one established class barrier was symptomatic of a general change in society's regard for the customary class distinctions, and the shedding of old snobberies and prejudices, though the suspicion is strong that the reasons for the change were materialistic rather than idealistic: trade unionism meant power. However that may have been, very soon the unions were catering for the professions, for managers and administrators, for airline pilots and scientific staffs. The face and style of the movement had changed radically.

So, after a beginning some seventy years ago in the suffering and travail of the humblest of the country's work force, trade unionism has spread outwards and upwards to such an extent that one must wonder whether the old ideology – if indeed it remains intact – will be strong enough to bind so many disparate and sometimes conflicting interests into a workable unity, without a considerable re-structuring of the decision-making processes and a greater willingness to submit to disciplines which are designed for mutual benefit and for the welfare of the greatest number.

Trade unionism now involves many thousands of members who have come comparatively late into the movement to avail of loyalties and practices which were evolved for mutual protection, welfare, and advancement when times and conditions were very different, and where the issues were, for the most part, basic ones, having to do more often than not with depressed wage levels, long working hours, insecure employment and inadequate holidays. The issues of today are seldom so fundamental.

The three principal weapons of trade unionism – the picket line, the sympathetic strike and the concept of 'tainted goods' which have survived almost unchanged from that earlier period – now have an application over a far wider area of industrial life. They are weapons that are open to exploitation by the unscrupulous. Even when used legitimately there have been instances of selfish abuse in which the scale of hardship and suffering inflicted on fellow trade unionists and the public has been out of all proportion to the petty grievances they set out to rectify, so much so that Congress a few years back found it necessary to revise the rules for picketing in order to limit this kind of casual exploitation of the deep-seated loyalties of workers not directly involved. A proportion of the disruption, justifiable or not, can be attributed to the obduracy of a managerial class who – certainly in the public sector – are going to continue to be paid their salaries however frequent the strikes in their concerns and however long they may last. Nevertheless, the manner and extent of the use of the traditional weapons in varying situations would seem to require serious consideration once again.

Much of the unrest which leads to industrial action today seems to centre on the question of differentials – the preservation of relativities – as though differentials and their preservation, in no matter what circumstances, was a trade union principle. This, in effect, tends to lead to sectionalism and to elitism, and consequently to rivalries and disunion. I remember some years back, a general agreement was reached which was to give a pound a week increase to those on salaries of less than £1200 a year but nothing to those earning over that amount. The idea was to give a special lift to the low wage earner and also to make the pound a real increase by avoiding the steeper rise in the cost of living which would occur if the increase was given generally. The pound was given, but the advantage was very soon wiped out by a wave of claims for the restoration of differentials. I remember wondering at the time how, if differentials must invariably be preserved, is the situation of the worker who has been badly paid from the start ever to be remedied? And is the badly-paid worker to be expected to approve an outlook which can only help to perpetuate the badly-paid worker's own disadvantaged place in the earnings league? It is an area where there should be some agreed procedures for singling out and nominating special cases.

Trade unionism in Ireland has come through three stages,

the first being its fight for recognition, both legally and industrially. In its second, its function was seen only in its relationship with the individual employer. Today it is part of the economic trio, that of employers as a body, of government, and of trade unions, with a say in national pay levels, social welfare structures, income tax policies and job creation. The recognition that all these interrelate to determine living standards throughout society as a whole has been urged by the trade unions for some time. Its recent acceptance can be expected to bring about further changes in a movement which has developed beyond recognition over the past twenty years.

(1979)

Jim Larkin – A Memoir

My first attempt to see Jim Larkin ended in disaster. It was in 1938 when I was a clerk in the Gas Company. After a good deal of persuasion a few of us had managed to convince the rest that the material benefit of being members of his Union would outweigh the superior social standing which in the thirties went with wearing a collar and tie and pushing a pen. So, on a sunlit summer's evening after work two of us set off for Unity Hall which stood (or, rather, staggered – it was in the extremities of decay) opposite the Pro-Cathedral. But as we crossed from O'Connell Bridge to Bachelor's Walk a fool of a cyclist with a pane of glass under one arm brushed against my friend and we had to head instead for Jervis Street Hospital. The gash in his hand had to have several stitches.

Next time we made it. There was a bare hallway leading to a bare staircase and a room with bare floorboards and a rough wooden table at which, under a bare electric light bulb suspended from its cobwebbed cord, the Man Himself was seated. He was tall, heavily built and obviously of great physical strength, with a lock of white hair that fell down over his forehead and a large, bent pipe which required vast quantities of matches to keep it up to the mark. In no time at all the matter of our joining his Union was lost among a hundred and one things besides: a welter of notions, topics and opinions that seemed to offer themselves in a ceaseless flow to that powerhouse of ideas which, I soon found out, was Jim Larkin's mind.

The accent was a strange mixture of Liverpool and Dublin, with now and then an echo of his years in America. He was then around sixty-two, in good shape physically for his age, but with a face much lined by hardship, long and bitter battles, and the constant wear and tear of his passionately held convictions. Marlborough Street in those days, I well remember, exuded that odour of decay and deep poverty which was the inescapable breath of Dublin's tenement world. Unity Hall was no exception. Its rooms exhaled that same smell and, through it, summoned the ghost of far-off days of suffering and struggle. It smelled of hunger, deprivation, disease. It spoke of a dogged if down-at-heel heroism by then long in the past.

We were admitted into membership and I got to know something about Larkin: his sudden and almost ungovernable outbursts of fury: his unpredictability; his unstoppable flights of oratory when he warmed to a theme. But there was also his tenderness towards the weak and unfortunate and his almost feminine sensitivity to human suffering. There were the amusing and everyday sides to his character too. He played cards quite a lot with his old time butties and hated so much to lose that he was not beyond using underhand means to avoid it. And, at a public meeting, if he paused briefly while speaking to cover his mouth with his handkerchief, I knew he was about to let an enormous Larkin roar out of him and was taking out his teeth first as a precaution against accidents.

In 1946 I became a Branch Secretary with him and a full time union employee. He was then in his seventies, I in my twenties and the youngest member of his staff, so he treated me with an old man's indulgence. An inner door connected his office with mine and he often stopped in to chat and smoke his pipe. That was in Thomas Ashe Hall in College Street which at that time had a busy bus terminus at its entrance. He told me he had plans to turn the ground floor of the Hall into a cafe so that the working-class mothers coming into town (usually with their children) for their shopping would have a place to rest in over a cup of tea or coffee. He died before it could be done and then, as with all organisations, office requirements expanded to eat up the spare accommodation and that was that. I realised that Larkin wanted for the underprivileged not just material sufficiency, but access to culture and the graces of living as well.

He was a man, as Sean O'Casey once said, who wanted a bowl of flowers on the table along with the loaf of bread. He would quote Shelley and Walt Whitman as a matter of course and took an active interest in cultural events of every kind. He was the prime mover, I remember, in having the freedom of the city of Dublin offered to Bernard Shaw and, indeed, the influence which persuaded that unpredictable sage of Synge Street to accept it. On one occasion at a Feis Ceoil competition for school orchestras I looked around to find the source of a bout of highly enthusiastic applause (one did not expect applause at a Feis Ceoil competition in those days) and saw that the source was Jim Larkin. A few seats to his right, incidentally, was the poet Paddy Kavanagh. In less elevated moods, he would ask the cashier for a shilling from the petty cash (he gave away most of his money) and slip over to a matinee at the Royal or the Regal. Why he bothered about the shilling I don't know. They always let him in free.

By that time, of course, the era of high heroics, the 'mad hooves galloping in the sky' had passed. From the time of his re-election to the newly constituted Dublin Corporation in 1931 he had devoted much of his energy to the problem of working-class housing. Tenements he hated, regarding them as a demoralising influence which wage increases and improved working conditions could never wipe out. So it was that three of the largest estates of working-class housing were linked with his direct efforts. Croydon Park had belonged to his Union before it was bought by the Corporation. Ellenfield Estate (Unity Park) was rented by his Union and held by him for city housing until the Corporation was in a position to buy it over. The acquisition of St Anne's Estate was largely due to his promptness in acting on a secret tip-off that it was about to be sold. He talked to the City Manager and a sum of money was found which was sufficient to buy a week's option and to give time for a meeting to be held before the option expired. The Corporation was able to buy it for £60,000.

Indeed, by 1946, the last year of his life (he died in January 1947) one of the regular sights of Dublin was Larkin on his journeys to and from the City Hall and Thomas Ashe Hall, usually in the company of another huge man and lifelong friend who had battled through more disputes than could be listed, Alderman Barney Conway. I watched them departing many a time from a window high up in Thomas Ashe Hall, two ageing battleships of a great revolutionary era, both full of good talk and intrepid courage, both life-long servants to the class they had sprung from, and both quite unconscious of the fact that they had hardly a shilling between them. That was well over thirty years ago. In the long years between I have met no men who were better.

(1979)

O'Casey and the Trade Unions

In a letter from his home in London to Horace Reynolds dated 6 February 1938, Sean O'Casey mentioned a recent visit from the labour leader, Jim Larkin and said, among other things: 'I had him with me the other evening with a friend and we talked from early evening to the coming of the morn.'

As, indeed, they would have. Both O'Casey and the veteran trade union leader were nearing their sixties, both were unstoppable talkers with a weakness for reminiscence, and both had shared together in the traumatic social and political upheavals which give the first two decades or so of Irish life in the twentieth century their strange mixture of pride and poverty, hunger, heroism and poltroonery and an elusive and scattered kind of grandeur. They had plenty to talk about. They would have talked of their mutual involvement in strikes and lock-outs, of rallies and gun-running, of foodships and soup kitchens and massive confrontations with law and religion. And, of course, of the personalities who had dominated the public imagination of the period. Many years later O'Casey, writing of these days, admitted that four buildings of the Dublin of those times remained, as he put it, forever in his heart and mind. They were his home, the church of St Barnabas, the Abbey Theatre and Liberty Hall.

Liberty Hall had been the centre of the working-class revolt against degrading conditions and, in considerable measure, of revolutionary nationalism, two movements which, as both men prophesied, were to prove incompatible.

After his father's death in middle life, O'Casey, who was six years old, came to know the worst horrors of Dublin's tenement life and the extremes of its hunger and poverty. He was the last born of thirteen children, eight of whom had died, a normal enough ratio in a city where the infant mortality rate was higher than Calcutta, then a plague spot. He was a sickly child, with a disease of the eyes, contracted from his unhygienic surroundings, which kept him from regular schooling and plagued him all his life. 'Poverty, pain and penance,' he was to write later, 'those were the gates of Dublin – its three castles.'

Religion pervaded his childhood, the more so perhaps because he was a Protestant child sharing to the full the deprivation of his predominantly Catholic neighbours. So too did the theme of war. As a young boy he saw his brothers and their friends going off in their colourful uniforms to fight the little, far-flung wars of Empire, and the songs of the household were those of the loyal soldiers of the Queen: 'Over the burning sands of Egypt,' for instance, or 'Goodbye Dolly I must leave you.' Yet in spite of extreme poverty and a traditional attachment to the Crown, his first adult enthusiasm was neither for trade unionism nor Union Jacks but, surprisingly, for the ideals, even the excesses, of the Gaelic Revival. He adopted with enthusiasm the Celtic symbols of the harp and the round tower; he read with excitement about High Kings and kings not so high; he learned to speak Irish as best he could and fell in love with traditional Irish music. He even learned to play the bagpipes in a sort of a way and became founder and secretary of the St Laurence O'Toole Pipers' Band. As a member of the Gaelic League he gaelicised his name to Seán O Cáthasaigh. He then joined the Irish Republican Brotherhood and took a hand in the militaristic euphoria of the times by trying his skill at patriotic verse. It was as outrageously banal as the general run of such work:

Beneath thy flag fresh hopes we feel
Ireland, dear Ireland
We'll gild its folds with glint of steel
And rifles' flame, dear Ireland.
In garish day, in night's damp dew
Its green and white and orange hue
Shall signal death to England's crew
And hope to thee, dear Ireland.

O'Casey could laugh at that later and write about it in self derision:

He glanced at the little, smoky lamp and fancied that it
had changed to a candle − a tall, white, holy candle, its
flame taking the shape of a sword; and, in its flaming point,
the lovely face of Cathleen, the daughter of Houlihan.

Though he meant every word of it at the time, his everyday experience of the Gaelic League began to erode his faith in it, particularly its failure to stand up to the influence and pressures of the Catholic clergy. He saw its Portarlington Branch collapse when the local clergy objected because it was teaching Irish to mixed classes. Crossroad dances also met with disapproval and were abandoned. There were attacks on publications such as Ryan's *The Irish Peasant*. And he was bitterly upset at their failure to stand up for Dr O'Hickey of Maynooth when he was dismissed for supporting the movement to have Irish as an essential subject in the new university.

As for the IRB and their patriotic songs and stances, these, he decided, were mainly impractical daydreams − all guns and drums, as he was to put it, and no wounds. They were lost and dreaming in the romantic ecstasy of Thomas Davis's:

O for a steed, a rushing steed, on the Curragh of Kildare
And Irish squadrons skilled to do what they are ready
    to dare
A hundred yards, and England's guards
Drawn up to engage me there.

That was a bit too fustian for the realist in O'Casey. Besides, the Republican movement attracted the middle and lower middle classes in the main, not the general labourer. Few of the Republicans were of his kinship. His genuine brethren, he decided, were in the tottering houses among the poverty and the decay.

Needless to say, no man sheds one set of ideals totally on one day and replaces them with an entirely new set the next. There is overlapping, there is blending, there is a period when the new ideals are the unconscious motivation to action while the old ones seem still to rule the will and the mind. And so it seems to have been with O'Casey, until two events occurred which rooted out the old ideas finally and gave ascendancy to the new. The first of these was his discovery of the plays and prefaces of Bernard Shaw. The second and more immediate to the Dublin situation was the advent of Jim Larkin and the consequent massive eruption of trade union feeling. O'Casey set out the situation in a letter which will be found in the first volume of David Krause's work, *The Letters of Sean O'Casey 1910-1941*. It is the letter to Horace Reynolds quoted earlier in which there is the reference to Larkin's visit. Dated 6 February 1938, it reads:

I had been for a good number of years a member of the Irish Republican Brotherhood and an ardent nationalist. Then came the preaching of Jim Larkin and the books of Bernard Shaw. (By the way, it was a young Dublin nation-alist named Kevin O'Loughlin, member of the third order of St Francis, who introduced me to Shaw, by persuading me to read the sixpenny edition of John Bull's Other Island). These two great men swung me over to the left and I became critical of pure nationalism. But, still more was I critical of the workings of the IRB. It was making no progress, and appealed only to clerks and artisans – the great body of workers were set aside. Hardly a man of them knew how to use a hack or shovel, and nothing about the building of defences. But particularly I hated

Bulmer Hobson, who was the white haired boy of Tom Clarke. Once Tom put me out of his shop because I criticised Hobson as Leader, and as Editor of Irish Freedom: Tom telling me he loved Bulmer as his own son.

The IRB took every help they could get (and they got a lot) from Jim Larkin's Union, and I did most of the work, for Jim was very fond of me . However, at a general meeting of the IRB in Dublin I criticised its working. I was howled at by a lot, and supported by some; Bulmer, on the platform, drew a gun and there was pandemonium. So afterwards, with some others, I left the IRB and flung myself into the Labour Movement, though still doing all I could for the National movement and for P.H. Pearse's school St Enda and the St Laurence O'Toole's Hurling and Football Club and Pipers' Band, which I founded and brought to a fine band with the help of chums. . . .

The Larkin influence on O'Casey was the more immediate. Jim Larkin had come to Dublin in 1908 to organise the unskilled and casual workers of the city, the dockers, the carters and the factory workers. These were working long hours for starvation wages and lived for the most part in the appalling conditions of the tenement ghettoes of the city. Larkin, whose energy and oratory were unique, soon had them banding together to challenge the employers in strike after strike and O'Casey, who had been working since 1903 as a general labourer with the Great Northern Railway of Ireland, joined Larkin's Union in 1911. In December of that year he was dismissed from his job, no reason being given officially.

The story is that he had been overheard attacking conditions in the railway and praising Jim Larkin's aggressive methods. He wrote a number of letters to the company requesting the reason for his dismissal and when the company declined to give reasons he published the correspondence in Larkin's paper, the *Irish Worker*. He was soon contributing regularly to its columns. Krause points to a letter of his urging workers to attend St Enda's to see a pageant produced by Pearse as one of many of his efforts to unite Labour and Nationalism. The letter is dated 7 June 1913. In August of that year the epic chain of events began that quenched any lingering desire of his to reconcile the two.

A tram strike called by Larkin developed into a wholesale lock-out which dragged on for over six months and involved about a third of the city. O'Casey, already unemployed, flung himself into the struggle. He worked in the food kitchens which were set up in the basement of Liberty Hall; he became secretary of the Women and Children's Relief Fund and later secretary of the Irish Citizen Army. He travelled the streets of Dublin in a borrowed horse and cart collecting funds and wrote several appeals for the pages of the *Irish Worker*.

As the lock-out dragged on and the poor suffered and starved, O'Casey's disillusionment with nationalism and, in particular, with the Irish Volunteers, became total. In January 1914 he wrote an open letter to workers in the Volunteers which began with a quote from John Mitchell: 'In a word, we demand Ireland for the Irish, not for the gentry alone.'

It was a sentiment which became basic to the thinking of both Larkin and O'Casey. 'Workers,' O'Casey wrote, 'do you not think it is high time to awake from your sleep and yield allegiance to no movement that does not avow the ultimate destiny of the workers?'

In response to the Volunteers' declared determination 'to secure and maintain the liberties and rights common to all Irishmen', O'Casey answered cynically:

We know the liberties and rights we enjoy: the right to toil till the blood is dried in our veins; the right to bless the land that gives us what it thinks we are worth; the right to suffer starvation, and misery, and disease, and then thank God that such light afflictions work an exceeding weight of glory. Workers, ye are fools to train and drill for anything less than complete enfranchisement, for the utter alteration of the present social system. . . .

His bitterness led to a clash with Countess Markiewicz, who

was involved in both the Volunteers and the Citizen Army. O'Casey's case was that among the leadership of the Volunteers were employers who had locked out union members during the 1913 lock-out and he tabled a motion at a meeting of the Citizen Army Council calling on her to sever her connection either with the Volunteers or the Citizen Army. His motion was defeated by one vote and O'Casey, in spite of Larkin's plea to the contrary, resigned as secretary, although he continued to write for the Army in the Irish Worker. Later, when he came to set out his thinking in a booklet called *The Story of the Irish Citizen Army* published by Maunsell & Company in 1918, he was more than ever convinced of the incompatibility of the Volunteer mentality and the aspirations of the trade union movement. He was also very conscious of the popular swing to the nationalistic stance of Sinn Fein which the 1916 Rising and the executions of the leaders had brought about even among the general labourers and the casual workers: 'The activities of Sinn Fein are spreading over the land,' he wrote, 'and Labour comes halting very much behind.'

He charged that Irish Labour propaganda was written from an English point of view and that its leaders were, as he put it, 'painfully ignorant of their country's history, language and literature.' Persecution had deepened the people's sympathy with their Irish origin and Irish labour leaders would have to take the change into account if they were to win over the working class. Ultimately, he concluded, Labour would have to fight Sinn Fein. In the event, Labour backed off. O'Casey could do little about it and Larkin, who might have, was locked up in Sing Sing prison for subversive activities. By the time of his release and return to Ireland in 1923, the Civil War had so politicised public thinking that social change was relegated to the back seats, where it remained for a generation.

Meanwhile, the Irish Transport & General Workers' Union, in the absence of Larkin in the United States, and his subsequent imprisonment there, had been built up and reorganised. One of the factors in its success was its involvement in the preparations for the insurrection of 1916 and its subsequent association with James Connolly who had become one of the executed leaders. On the new union executive were men who considered Larkin too rash and too self-willed to be given the free hand with decisions he had had in the past. They were not at all enthusiastic about the idea of his return to Ireland. The leader of this school of thought was William O'Brien, general treasurer of the Union in 1919.

O'Casey was now Honorary Secretary of the Jim Larkin Correspondence Committee, which had been set up to organise a massive Christmas greeting from Irish workers to Larkin in Sing Sing. William O'Brien ignored O'Casey's request for an interview about the greeting and, presumably, declined to sign the greeting himself. O'Casey also describes in *Inishfallen Fare Thee Well* how he attempted to get the Dáil to call collectively for Larkin's release, but the Treaty debate was at its height and unleashing hatreds which excluded everything other than themselves. The terrible beauty, O'Casey remarked, was beginning to lose her good looks. Cathleen Ni Houlihan had become, as he put it, 'oul snarley gob.'

Trade unionism was soon to follow the nationalists' bad example. When Larkin returned to Ireland in 1923 a quarrel broke out between himself and the Executive Committee which resulted eventually in a court case, and his expulsion from the union he had founded. His followers then set up a breakaway union, The Workers' Union of Ireland. Who was to blame for the course of events is not of much importance today, though Larkin himself must bear his share. What is worth remarking is that the seeds of the quarrel existed as far back as 1911. Correspondence between James Connolly and William O'Brien, published later on in O'Brien's book *The Attempt to Smash the Irish Transport & General Workers' Union*, shows O'Brien encouraging Connolly's resentment of Larkin's almost total control of affairs. At the Trade Union Congress of 1914, under Larkin's presidency, there were muted clashes between O'Brien and Larkin, a rift which time failed to heal.

In O'Casey's eyes, the victory of the O'Brien faction over Larkin represented the triumph of compromise in the class struggle, over a leader who saw trade unionism as a militant and revolutionary movement which would change the world. The impact of Larkin's first appearance on the Dublin scene on O'Casey is described in the autobiographies: 'Here was a man who would put a flower in a vase on a table as well as a loaf on a plate. Here, Sean thought, is the beginning of a broad and busy day.'

Larkin's vision of trade unionism was one of a working class with access not only to the necessities of food, and work, and shelter but to all the graces of living: to music and poetry and pictures, to the countryside and the seaside, to education and intellectual pursuits. It was a vision that excited O'Casey so much that he adopted it as his own. Nobody else but Larkin, he felt, could achieve it for the poor of Ireland. Certainly, in O'Casey's eyes, not the O'Briens of his world. The thought was still with him when he paid tribute to Larkin on the Labour leader's death in 1947: 'He was the first man in Ireland,' O'Casey wrote in the *Irish Times,* 'who brought poetry into the workers' fight for a better life.' And it had been with him earlier, or so he asserts, when he was packing up to leave Ireland in disgust in 1926. He writes in *Inishfallen Fare Thee Well* – and the sense of loss is still there:

> Sean packed his last few personal things into his one suitcase, the suitcase that had gone with him to Coole and was now to shepherd the things that would allow him to strut respectably through the streets of London. There was nothing to keep him in Ireland: he had no part in Cosgrave's Party, or in de Valera's policy; nor had he any in a Labour movement bossed by William O'Brien.

It was O'Casey's farewell, not only to Inishfallen, but to active membership of the union, although he would certainly continue to champion working-class causes all his long life. The truth was that his true star had been rising in another point of the heavens. Even during the trade union split on Larkin's return in 1923 he had the first production of *The Shadow of a Gunman* at the Abbey to fill his mind and fire his ambitions, and *Juno and the Paycock* already taking shape in his imagination, so that his letters are more and more concerned with the business of playwriting, and hardly at all with the themes of political and social change. These issues, together with mankind's right to happiness and merriment and total freedom of choice, were to be presented as themes for drama. The redistribution of emphasis can be seen in a letter he wrote to Lady Gregory in January of 1925, asking her permission on Jim Larkin's behalf to stage *The Rising of the Moon* at a union concert in the Queen's. Permission was granted. Indeed, I remember young Jim Larkin giving an account of his father's performance in it. Big Jim Larkin held the view that there was no necessity to learn lines: he felt they would come naturally and spontaneously to him in the excitement of performance. The result, I understand, was hilarious, though it had little to do with Lady Gregory's play.

It was natural, of course, that O'Casey's experiences of trade unionism should get into his plays, just as did his political involvements and the events of his formative years. *The Star Turns Red* and *Red Roses for Me* are two specific examples, though *The Star Turns Red* is about the conflict between fascism and communism rather than the trade union struggle. It has Comrade Chief Red Jim in it, of course, and there is an all-out attempt by the police and the saffron shirts to break a strike, together with an attempt to betray Jim by union officials which may have remote roots in the Dublin split of 1923, but it does not absorb and reflect back truly O'Casey's experience of the Dublin trade union upheavals of 1908-1914.

In *Red Roses for Me*, which, in addition, contains a fair amount of autobiography, the picture is closer to his real trade union experience, and the dialogue and characterisation are more effective and evocative of what surrounded him in those Dublin days. Certainly the aspirations expressed by the hero Ayamonn sound very much like those which flowered in O'Casey himself and which remained to inspire much of what he subsequently wrote.

And what, ultimately, did he get from his trade union

experiences? First, perhaps, a wholesome rejection of a nationalistic will-o-the-wisp which favoured revolution, provided everyone in society continued to know his place. Second, a devotion to every 'ism' of the Left which was so uncritical and unanalytical that it could become at times both tedious and shrill. Lastly and most important, trades unionism and nationalism and the Gaelic Revival were sources which supplied a gallery of characters behaving at their all-out worst or best. They surrounded him and reacted to him and he got the measure of them all: a bevy of narrow-minded, craw-thumping, mendacious and self-seeking middle-of-the-road men; a galaxy of underprivileged Joxers and Fluthers and Coveys and Brennans-of-the-Moor, who were not entirely incapable of lapses into nobility, and who used a sort of boastful fantasy as a defence against the unremitting insults of a contemptuous and uncaring society; and women of heroism and fortitude and instinctive compassion. And, in addition to all that, a personal view of humankind which remained at bottom undefeatable, ever-hopeful and ever-aspiring. In the end, the gain surely repaid the suffering.

(1980)

4

The Short Story

In creative short story writing, technique is almost entirely organic, by which I mean that it is inherent in the effort at expression itself. It arises from the writer's struggle with his material and is not imposed from without. There *is* a technique, of course, which *can* be imposed from without. We find it in the magazine type of story, for instance. People who write magazine stories work to their own rules. First of all they study the markets, as they call it. This means working out what the editor of a particular magazine favours and then trying to write to that order. They make notes like this:

Wendy's Magazine:
Readership: Girls and the newly married – better class.
Themes favoured: Light Romantic/Domestic subjects, middleclass background. Also childhood themes, especially for summer season with country cottage or seaside background. Also Country Doctor/village setting. Domestic pets occasionally. Happy ending essential. Best length 1500-2000 words (approx.)
Rates 3 guineas per thousand.

So, with this basic information at their disposal, the magazine writers go off looking for plots which will give them material for 1500-2000 words (approx.), and, as for technique, that is something which they supply according to a formula which, in itself, has been extracted from a close study of the market, which means a close imitation of what every other writer published in *Wendy's Magazine* has been doing.

Writing magazine stories of this kind is something that can be learned by application, if we have the inclination and a little aptitude for it. Music can be written in the same way. Ebenezer Prout's textbook on the art of fugue, for instance, will teach any industrious student how to turn out fugues by the dozen, well-made fugues, fugues better from the point of view of the Rules of Fugue than most of Bach's. But neither the fugues nor the stories made in this way have a life of their own, and they don't engage us except at the most superficial level. And the reason is that as readers we are not making contact with anyone or anything, because the writer of the magazine story himself had no personal involvement with the situation he portrays or with his characters.

Creative writing, on the other hand, even bad creative writing, is creative precisely because is *is* involved. The creative writer struggles to express the human condition as he personally sees it. His reaction to life and to people may be compassionate and sympathetic; it may be one of disgust and rejection; he may express himself in terms of realism or of fantasy – it doesn't greatly matter. What does matter is that life has compelled him to involve himself in an act which is one of self-expression. And, if he succeeds in self expression, we are likely to be interested. Why? I don't really know. Perhaps at some point our understanding became darkened; perhaps it is that we are all possessed of souls that at some time or other lost their tongues, and ever since have been struggling to become articulate again. So that, when a man of genius becomes articulate in that spiritual sense through music or literature, or of the arts, we feel that we too have been granted the blessing and relief of speech.

So then, in creative writing, as in every other art, there is this effort to be articulate. It involves a struggle with words, with form, with imagination and even with the inconsistent promptings of the human mind, which tells the writer that if he wants any peace, he'd better give over all this daydreaming and sit down and struggle with the task before him. Then, of course, when he's sitting down it warns him that all this physical inactivity is very bad for him and that he'd be much better off having a walk in the fresh air or even a few pints at the local.

At this point, we'd better assume that the writer stays put, because it brings us to a consideration of the problem before him, which Sean O'Faolain has described as 'the technical struggle'. We are assuming, by the way, that the writer has a subject to struggle with, because the technical struggle, in O'Faolain's analysis, has four elements. These are:

1. Convention
2. Subject
3. Construction
4. Language

Out of the interaction of these four will arise The Technique and that is why I spoke at the beginning of a technique which is organic – that is, inherent in the material itself. To illustrate briefly my use of the words organic and formal here, let me describe a Sonnet as formal in technique because the form is pre-determined and 'The Wasteland' by T.S. Eliot as organic, because the subject matter eventually supplies the shape.

The first of O'Faolain's elements of technique, convention, is easy enough to get to grips with, because literary convention has been developing for so many hundreds of years now that even people who make no great study of reading are aware of it. It is no longer necessary, in order to alert the reader to the fact that a story is about to be unfolded, to begin with: 'Once upon a time, and a very good time it was' or the same thing with a bit of a brogue added: 'Let you stir up the fire now, and draw in the creepy stool, 'til I tell you about the quare woman that lived long ago in the glen of the rowan trees, not three Irish miles from the village your father himself (the light of heaven to him) was born in.'

You could, of course, begin a story in that way today, but

you'd have to have a very good technical reason for it, (for example Mary Lavin's 'The Story of the Widow's Son'), whereas long ago you'd cause a great deal of confusion if you began it any other way. It was the convention then – it isn't today. Today's story needn't begin at the beginning. It can start at the middle like O'Connor's story, 'Guests of the Nation', or at the end, or long past the end, like McLaverty's 'The Poteen Maker' or anywhere it chooses to start. It can start:

> Crash!
> The bedclothes were thrown back, his feet found the floor. The switch? He felt about the wall until light flooded the room. Nothing now. Absolute silence. Was there to be another night of it? And so far from help.
> 'I believe it is,' Carmody said, regarding his brandy and soda, the old sundowner.
> 'Nonsense.'
> 'Everybody says that,' Carmody said, 'until they try it.' He glanced at his watch. Midnight.
> 'About now,' he mused. 'Yes – just about now.'

There are several pieces of information conveyed in that passage provided you understand the convention. My mother, I'm certain, and in the matter of literature she's a very simple and unsophisticated woman, would take all that in her stride; whereas the great Dr Johnson, I'm equally certain, would be utterly confounded and at a loss to extract any meaning whatever from it. And that is because the reader today accepts and understands a convention of compression undreamed of in the eighteenth century. The same thing has happened in music. The opening of Beethoven's *Seventh Symphony* nearly prostrated the critics of his time because he didn't prepare and resolve his discords the way convention ordained and as they felt they had a right to expect. Today we have grown to understand the Beethoven convention and we take his use of musical form in our stride.

Let me go back to the illustration for a moment to examine how far along the road of compression we have travelled:

Crash!

The bedclothes were thrown back, his feet found the floor. *The Switch?* He *felt about the wall* until light flooded the room. Nothing now. Absolute silence. *Was there to be another night of it?* And *so far from help.*

'I believe it is,' Carmody said, regarding his brandy and soda, the old sundowner.

'Nonsense.'

'Everybody says that,' Carmody said, 'until they try it.' He glanced at his watch. Midnight!

'About now,' he mused 'Yes – just about now.'

In the space of two short paragraphs two locations are dealt with, three characters are introduced, suspense is created and an atmosphere of mystery.

Compression, then, is an aspect of the short story, acceptable because the convention is understood. Its acceptance has helped enormously in the development of the short story as a form: it helps it, for instance, to be short, by making lengthy descriptions of people and places unnecessary, and allowing a piece of business, an innuendo, the crack of a twig, the glint of sunlight on a rifle barrel, to stand for a great forest, broiling sun, dried up undergrowth, a search, a moment of alertness and danger.

But there is a lot more to convention than compression. The writer and the reader are both enormously influenced by the society they live in, by current ideas on art, philosophy, literature; ideas on conduct, ideas on man's nature, ideas on man's destination – or lack of it. No individual can stand completely apart from the outlook of the age he lives in, least of all the writer, who, if he is to fulfil his creative function, which as I suggested earlier is to give a tongue to his age, must reflect his age and show it in microcosm in his work. He can only communicate by keeping in and around the convention even if he is being iconoclastic and even if he is trying to develop and expand the boundaries of accepted technique. The literary convention will have a mode imposed on it by the age he lives in, from which he will find it very difficult to depart. Every age has imposed its outlook on its literature.

In the sixteenth century, for instance, it was the fashion to wear the heart on the sleeve: to give free rein to the expression of emotions, particularly those evoked by love, envy, hate, revenge; and by the then universal acknowledgment of the mystery and enormity of Death. The eighteenth century, on the other hand, wore a mask. Its ideal was control, intellect, good taste as expressed by Cowper, Walpole, Dr Johnson, Swift and Pope. It pinned its faith on the cultivated mind, and believed in grace and precision in the expression of ideas and in the value of intellectual control as a measurement of man. Frank O'Connor has pointed out that we can get a compelling picture of Shakespeare's greatness by reading his works, while knowing little or nothing about the details of his life; whereas to flavour even Swift fully – and Swift was an unusually passionate writer for his age – we must know something more, something of the small politics and interesting personalities of the society he lived in. If Swift were alive to-day he would express his fiery personality in the convention of today.

The nineteenth century spent most of its time scrutinising man as a social animal. The rise of the Chartist Movement and the writings of Marx resulted eventually in the iconoclasm of Samuel Butler, the scathing social criticisms of Ibsen and Shaw. Man, as the writers saw him, was descended from the lower orders of creation and his society was different from that of the ant and the bee only in being less perfectly organised. The metaphysical element in man's make-up sank right down to the bottom of the barrel.

I have run over this ground briefly to establish what you will, I think, accept. A writer must be of his own age. He cannot now write as Shakespeare did or as Pope did or as did the great novelists of the nineteenth century. His technique is limited by the literary convention of his times.

And now let us look at subject. Subject is the most personal element in the art of writing and yet the least important from the point of view of self-expression. Jonathan Swift, as we know, could write about a broomstick. To come to our own times, O'Flaherty's 'The Three Lambs' is so simple in its story content as at first sight to be hardly a subject at all. In Frank O'Connor's 'The Majesty of the Law' the subject is as ordinary as it could possibly be: An old man refuses to pay a fine imposed on him for striking another old man in an argument and goes to gaol instead.

After writing that sentence I decided to glance quickly through 'The Majesty of the Law' in order to check my memory of it and I found that that is the story content. I also found I had to read it through to the end. And once again I have had the joy of looking at a piece of life through the eyes of genius. There is a whole world contained in the compass of this story: there is simplicity, dignity, courtesy, hospitality, humour, pride, wisdom. I have met and listened to two people, an old man and a police sergeant, two immortals who have been added to my world by the magic of literature and whom I know better than many people I meet every other day. And through knowing them I know more about man's dignity as a creature, and I have a new pride in belonging to the ancient culture that moulded the independence and nobility of this old peasant man. The simple situation, for reasons that he could probably not explain satisfactorily himself, unloosed the tongue of O'Connor's soul and endowed him with a moment of omniscience.

So, the size or length of a subject is of no great importance. What matters is its capacity to strike fire within the writer and then to release his creative flame. A writer never writes a story about a subject. He uses a subject in order to write Himself.

Subject is probably the most puzzling ingredient of all for a writer at the beginning of his apprenticeship, when he has all the inner disturbance of the writer to cope with and can find no means of releasing it. I remember this very well at school, when I had no subjects at all, and when I wanted to express something. I thought that a good start was to work in words like 'azure', 'darkling', 'gloaming', 'feathered friends' (meaning birds), 'silver-throated' (meaning any bird's singing, including birds that never sang since creation started) 'modern repast' (the navvy swigging tea from a can) and 'the great white horses of the ocean' when I meant waves. But I am straying away from subject into language.

Reading Corkery's story, 'The Breath of Life', the other day, I remembered sending a very early story of my own to O'Faolain when he was editing *The Bell*. It was all about a violinist starving in an attic because the world was blind to his gifts. The story dealt with his last few hours on earth, when he had decided to give up grubbing for money and sits down to play and play to the four walls of his room, until at last, from hunger and exhaustion, he collapses. As he passes out he knocks over the oil lamp and fiddler, attic and all go up in smoke.

The story had a remarkable effect on O'Faolain, because it moved him to scribble a comment on the manuscript when he sent it back, which read: 'Why am I always getting stories about damned fiddlers? This is the third this week.'

For a while I wondered how anyone so deficient in judgment and good taste could ever have made it as an editor, until with time I tumbled to a truth that all writers learn sooner or later: you can't manufacture material. That musician was a deplorable and romantic fake. So is Corkery's musician in 'The Breath of Life' by the way. As a subject he releases nothing, except a high-minded hallucination about mountains and music. Personally I think it a deplorable story and I hold it up as an example of the effect on a good writer of a bad choice of subject, because nothing that I can see of the genius of Corkery has managed to get into it. Compare it with the kind of vision that permeates 'Vanity'.

Let us pass on to Construction.

Construction is the way the story is built, the harmony of its parts, the graph of its interest. Construction is usually what we mean when we talk about technique, because the craft of writing is more immediately recognisable in it than in convention or subject or language. Construction is making the narrative flow, the action unfold without the reader becoming conscious of the convention. Any sudden flaw in construction and the illusion is shattered – the cat is out of the bag. Construction is the devil.

I remember a friend of mine who met Paddy Kavanagh when he was working on *Tarry Flynn*.

'And how's the novel going, Paddy?' asked the friend.

'Great,' said Paddy. 'Great, I'll have it finished any day now!'

And the friend expressed his pleasure at the news. A fortnight later he ran into Paddy again. Paddy was looking gloomy.

'And how's the novel?' the friend asked, more out of politeness than anything else.

'Terrible,' said Paddy. 'Terrible. I've this fella stuck in a field and I can't get him out of it.'

The passage of time, for example, within the restricted length of the short story can cause great technical problems. Transition must be made smoothly and delicately, so that incidents widely separated in time dovetail into each other almost unnoticed. Convention will no longer allow us the simple 'time passes' formulas of the silent cinema: 'Came The Dawn'; 'Meanwhile, back at the Ranch.' That sort of thing. I remember reading a story once in which this appeared: 'Twenty years passed. They were both much older.' You can see the writer's mind wasn't on his job.

Some stories will take the simplest construction possible, which is to begin at the beginning and follow the natural order of events right to the end, as O'Flaherty does with 'The Three Lambs'.

O'Connor could have done the same thing with 'The Majesty of the Law', starting with the two old men meeting in the village, going for a drink together perhaps; an argument developing to the point where one of them strikes the other; then the victim reporting the assault; then the court case and the imposition of the fine, with the alternative of imprisonment; then the sergeant calling to the old man and the old man refusing to pay the fine – and so on. There is nothing in that sort of A to Z treatment that O'Connor could not have handled with gusto. But instead he does something much more skilful.

The sergeant and the old man are forbidden to plunge into the heart of the business by the courtesies of country custom. Hospitality must be offered, neighbourly talk must be exchanged, the civilities must be observed. So they talk for most of the time about other things. The Irish approach everything obliquely. They seldom ask: 'What time is it?' They more often say: 'I suppose you wouldn't have the time on you.'

And because custom and innate courtesy forbid the sergeant and the old man from plunging with ignorant haste into the business of the evening, O'Connor holds up letting us know what the story is all about until almost the end. O'Connor tells us the story as an afterthought, as it were. Just as the sergeant mentions the real business of the visit as an afterthought. But in the meanwhile we have been entertained by the best of good company. So we don't mind. At the end we know O'Connor has been playing a trick on us, but it's a witty one, calculated to give emphasis to the oblique and tortuous usages of his characters, and we forgive him. The construction itself provides a deft illustration of the subject and because it does, it is as it is.

Earlier I mentioned compression as a part of convention. Now let me try to illustrate it as part of construction – as getting over the time-transition for instance. The story may require a love encounter (so many of them do) in the country – suppose – on an enchanted, moonlit night in summer. The encounter ends. Now let us try to bridge the gap between the moment of high emotion, and the reconsideration the next day – or even some months later. All right. The short story writer cannot hold up the action while he describes in detail the moon, the clouds, the great sweep of the star-studded sky: unless of course, such a description is necessary to the subject (perhaps the lovers are mutually interested in astronomy). For compression's sake he will be content to imply it all in his observation of something small: the glint of moonlight on the leaves of the ash tree the lovers are standing under; the reflection of a star in the pool of the river – and they both make a wish on it. In plain language, he'll make every image do double work.

And he'll use these – and even put them into his story when pushed – so that the transitions can be made with economy and with dexterity. He'll say: 'When the sun found the pool it was almost midday' to indicate a change from night to the next day. Or, changing the season, he'll say: 'The leaves scattered about the ash tree were lodged firmly in the frost-hardened ground.'

So, with economy of trappings and good use of them, and with the help of sweat and blood, he constructs. Construction, as I've said, can be the very devil.

There now remains the last element of technique: language. Already I've mentioned words that ought to be avoided – self-conscious literary words and phrases like 'frugal repast', 'waning moons', 'shy daises peeping from the verdant fields' – that sort of thing. These words and phrases are useful sometimes, for instance, when they are put in to guy the self-conscious speech or literary style of one of the characters, or as a device used deliberately for comic effect. Or as Joyce uses them in 'The House of Horne' episode when he ranges through the literary styles of hundreds of years as a counterpoint to the development from the embryo to the birth of the baby; or as Flann O'Brien does in the mock saga passages about Finn and Sweeny.

Language in the short story should harmonise not with the subject, but with the author's mood about his subject. It isn't necessary, when writing about peasant life, for example, to write in a peasant idiom. Although there are times when the author will decide that that is the very best way to do it.

Having discussed O'Faolain's four elements of the technical struggle – Convention, Subject, Construction, Language – the remaining question is: why does a writer write? My own view is that it is his attempt to understand his own memories. Memory, I firmly believe, is the source of all insight, and literature is conceived out of the constant contemplation of those images which accumulate in the memory and persist in making their presence felt throughout the whole of the writer's life. This interior life is the possession of each and every one, of us, but the writer nourishes it and listens to it within himself in a very special way: by withdrawal, contemplation and self-questioning – a procedure which is not as lunatic or odd as it sounds. Everybody with a spark of awareness and engagement contemplates and self-questions from time to time. The writer, when he writes, is only externalising the interior dialogue which goes on throughout his life. He is giving a tongue to his soul or, to put it another way, he is trying to bring forth on paper the fruits of what AE has called 'the exquisite soliloquy between himself and heaven'.

(1966)

On The Nature of Poetry . . .*

> True ease in writing comes from art, not chance
> As those move easiest who have learned to dance.

This couplet from Alexander Pope's 'An Essay on Criticism' conveys the notion that to write well a poet must learn the art of poetry, just as a dancer must learn something about dancing in order to dance well. And it follows that if we learn a little about the art of poetry or dancing — or any other art, for that matter — we will enjoy it more.

There are two things which strike one about that quotation. The first is that Pope was giving good advice to those of us who read poetry, which is that we'll enjoy it more and understand it more if we learn something about the art of poetry: if we spend some of our time considering what poetry is and how poets go about making a poem. The second is that when Pope wrote that couplet about how to write poetry, he himself wasn't writing poetry at all. If that seems a shockingly unmannerly thing to say about a genius such as Pope, I can only add that Wordsworth expressed more or less the same opinion about it too, and when everybody got over the shock, many people began to agree with him. They began to say to one another: What is poetry?

Before we try to answer that question here let's deal with

*This essay and the following three essays are talks on poetry given to young students for Teléfís Eireann.

another one first. Why poetry at all? What use is poetry? Isn't
there enough to be studied and struggled with in this short
life of ours without the addition of poetry? I suppose there
is. And while we're at it we might as well throw in painting
and singing and music and dancing. Why dance? Why sing?
Why paint? The answer is that we can't help it. We might
as well say why breathe, why eat, why grow? Men have been
dancing and singing and painting and making poetry since
the world began and they are likely to go on doing so until
the world ends, without asking leave or licence of those who
think these things a bit of a nuisance. For man, among other
things, is a creature of passion and imagination. And poetry
is the language of the imagination and the passions.

So we've arrived at one answer to the question: What is
Poetry? It is the language of the imagination and the passions.
William Hazlitt said that, by the way, in a talk he gave in 1818.
Poetry arises out of the kind of being man is. It exists of natural
necessity. Without poetry, Shakespeare observed, man's life
would be as poor as the beasts. He was taking it for granted,
you see, that a beast never feels poetry. I think he was wrong.
What about the way the dog behaves when the rain clears off
and you bring him for a walk after he has been hours locked
up in the house? What does he do? He chases the leaves
scurrying in the lane, he barks at his own shadow, he waves
his tail about like a flag at a football match when a goal has
been scored, he tries to sniff at ninety different things at once
- if dogs wore a hat I think he'd fling it high in the air.

To my mind that dog is in a state of poetic frenzy and his
behaviour is simply the way a dog goes about expressing his
poetry. Poetry, Robert Frost has said, begins in delight, which
means that people waving flags at a football match, or cheering
a brass band are all enjoying poetry.

If you think that that isn't poetry let me quote Hazlitt again:

> There is no thought or feeling that can have entered into
> the mind of man, which *he* would be eager to
> communicate to others, or which *they* would listen to with
> delight, that is not a fit subject for poetry. Fear is poetry,

hope is poetry, love is poetry, hatred is poetry; contempt, jealousy, remorse, admiration, wonder, pity, despair, or madness - are *all* poetry. Man is a poetical animal, and those of us who do not study the principles of poetry nevertheless act on them all our lives, like the character in Moliere's play who suddenly discovered in middle age that he been speaking prose all his life without knowing it.

The child is a poet when he first plays at hide and seek, or repeats the story of Jack the Giant Killer; the shepherd boy is a poet when he first crowns his mistress with a garland of flowers; the city apprentice when he gazes after the Lord Mayor's show; the miser when he hugs his gold.

The hero and the coward, the beggar and the king, the rich and the poor, the young and the old, all live in a world of their own making; and the poet does no more than describe what all the others think and act. If his art is folly and madness, it is the folly and madness of all mankind.

Hazlitt is right. Mankind is a bit foolish, a little bit mad. All of us. Think of the things we do. We go on a holiday and we save a piece of a train ticket as a memento of it. Or we pluck a sprig of heather when we climb a mountain and we keep it until it crumbles to dust, because somehow that piece of heather has trapped for our contemplation all the glory and joy of high hills and summer skies. A mother will cut a lock of her baby's hair and keep it until he grows a man – often very much to the grown man's embarrassment!

In Liam O' Flaherty's story, 'Going into Exile', the young son of the house, setting off for exile in America, prises a little flake of whitewash off the wall of the cottage with his nail and puts it carefully in his pocket. That flake of whitewash, that piece of a train ticket, the faded sprig of heather, and the lock of hair are all little poems – poems without words, as it were – that belong to the world Hazlitt spoke about, the world all of us carry within us, the world of our own making.

And that brings us to another Truth. We all live in two

worlds at the same time: the world outside us, and the world inside us. Poetry is the voice of the world inside us, the world which is shaped by our passions and our imagination. Let me give an example of these two worlds or, to put it another way, these two aspects of reality: the outer reality and the inner reality. In every tangible thing, that is to say, in everything we can touch, there is something which we cannot touch. Think of a chair. A chair is a very ordinary sort of thing, a common-or-garden piece of furniture, something to sit on. Yet when you consider it another way there's much more to a chair than that. A man in the darkening fields on a winter's evening, after working all day in the cold, will straighten his back and think of his chair at home at the fire. And that chair will mean ease, comfort, warmth, the tender solicitude of his wife, the love and affection of his children. He will see it as a retreat from the buffeting of the elements and the bruises of the world; he will see it as a place in which to dream. In its outer reality the chair at the fire is simply a chair. The chair in the inner reality of the man's mind is a poem, and if the man were a poet he might well write a poem about it. If he were a sensible poet, of course, he'd wait until he had his supper first.

So, there are two Realities: an outer world where only events happen; and an inner world of our own making, a world lit by the lamp of imagination, where the events and accidents of the outer world undergo a magical transformation and we are likely at any moment to be ambushed by a poem. Time and again in this inner world poetic experiences trouble and delight the human heart. But, where the rest of us are unable to put words to our intuitions and our visions, the poet's business is to get to the heart of these experiences, to put in words which communicate to others what others already know, but have found inexpressible. Shakespeare has described for us what it is the poet achieves:

> The poet's eye in a fine frenzy rolling
> Doth glance from heav'n to earth, from earth to heav'n
> And as imagination bodies forth

The forms of things unknown, the poet's pen
Turns them to shape, and gives their airy nothing
A local habitation and a name.

Music and dancing, just as much as poetry, are expressions
of the inner life of man. Primitive man didn't dance simply
for exercise or sing to air his lungs – or for that matter, if
he had a bad voice, to annoy his neighbours. He did these
things, as I have said, because he was a *man,* and because men,
feeling happiness and sorrow, terror and delight, had to share
these experiences with their fellow men and with one another
or go mad at being dumb.

That may be a bit hard to understand nowadays, when we
are surrounded most of the time by noise and distraction: by
television, radio, record players, cinemas, motor cars; and as
often as not, the terrible ugliness of large cities. How often
nowadays have we time for quietness and contemplation: time
in which to measure the sure changing of the seasons; to
observe the flight of the bird; to try to count the stars of the
heavens or to see in the way God has placed them in the sky
the fabulous shapes of beasts and demons? But that is what
our ancestors did, thousands of years ago. They looked at the
stars in one part of the sky and they said, trying to express
their wonder and their awe, trying to reduce that immensity
to human comprehension – to give it, as the poet said 'a local
habitation and a name' – they said to their neighbour,
pointing to the sky, 'Look, it's like a plough'. And they looked
in another part of the sky, and they said, 'It's a bear, it's a
great bear'. And they looked at a third and said, 'That star
has a red face. It must be angry'.

That is the beginning of poetry, the effort to express one
thing in terms of another: the effort to understand all things
in terms of their meaning in the heart and imagination of man.
Poetry begins in simile, metaphor and symbol, that is to say,
in imagery. In the same way men pondered on the life about
them and saw that nature herself moved to ordained patterns.
The seas rise and ebb and rise and ebb; the seed is sown and

ripens and is reaped and after an interval is sown again; the sun rises and sets, the moon waxes and wanes, the seasons follow in their unchanging order and man himself is born and grows and matures and dies and his children take the same unvarying road. Men saw that the whole world moves to the measure of a dance, and they, imitating it, trying to express it, to propitiate it, danced in their turn and discovered the power of rhythm to unlock the fear and wonder and elation in their hearts. So rhythm became part of poetic expression too, just as it is part of music and dancing and life itself.

It has been said that primitive man spoke poetry before he learned to speak prose. Certainly rhythm and imagery are as old as language itself and they have pleased men for hundreds and hundreds of years. Think of popular expressions:

> As fit as a fiddle
> As slow as a snail
> As cute as a fox
> As stubborn as a mule

Now add rhyme, which supplies a music of its own and serves the very practical purpose of helping people to memorise what has been said: 'Early to bed and early to rise, Makes a man healthy, wealthy and wise.' At this point, we have something which looks very like poetry. In a way it's a bit like Pope, without his genius and virtuosity. It appeals to our reason, it entertains because it is pithy. But does it work on our imagination? Does it engage our emotion? I don't think so. Now let's go a step further:

> There was a crooked man
> Who walked a crooked mile
> He found a crooked sixpence
> Against a crooked stile.
> He bought a crooked cat
> Which caught a crooked mouse
> And they all lived together
> In a little crooked house.

Now at last we have poetry: very simple, unsophisticated poetry – but poetry. It opens a window on the country of the imagination. That crooked man never existed in the world about us. He belongs, with his crooked cat and crooked mouse and his little crooked house, to the townland of Never-never. Could you describe the countryside through which he walked the crooked mile? It's an interior landscape – all in here in the head, to be seen only with what Wordsworth called in his poem on 'The Daffodils', 'the inward eye'. It has a wooden signpost, for a start; it has roads that try to go everywhere at once, crazy humpbacked bridges, a windmill somewhere, a castle with turrets somewhere, patchwork fields, and somewhere or other there's a little red hen and a white goose that lays golden eggs. I'm quite certain about that, because it's the country of fairy tales.

How does the verse achieve this effect? I think it's the placing of the man, the road, the stile, the sixpence, the cat, the mouse and the little house all in relation to the word crooked, and the way the repetition of that word makes the poem jog along in a merry and amusing sort of way.

Poets use words in that way to release emotions and, in more accomplished verses than those about the crooked man, to compress meaning and fill the mind with the pleasure of responding to several associations at once. Let's take the word 'crooked' again and see it achieving the very opposite effect to the one I've mentioned:

> The glories of our blood and state
> Are shadows, not substantial things
> There is no armour against fate.
> Death lays his icy hand on kings.
> Sceptre and crown
> Must tumble down
> And in the dust be equal made
> With the poor, crooked scythe and spade.

In that poem 'crooked' stands for several things at once – and none of them merry. It describes the shape of the scythe, which of course is crooked. It describes the humble people

who work with the scythe and are bent with labour. It conveys
pity for them – as we can see from the addition of the word
'poor': 'the *poor, crooked* scythe and spade'. Even that additional
word 'poor' is carrying two ideas at once: the thought that those
who use the scythe are poor in the sense of poverty, and the
thought that they are to be pitied, in the sense that we say 'my
poor man'; 'poor little chap'; 'ah, the poor thing'. That, of course,
is imagery. We know it isn't the crown that will tumble down,
but the man who wears it. We know the poet isn't concerned
simply because the scythe and the spade are going to crumble
and decay. He means the kind and simple people who earn
their livelihoods with them. And listen to the sound of the lines:

> Sceptre and crown
> Must tumble down

Can't you hear in them the rumble and collapse of the proud
palaces of kings? Robert Frost, I told you earlier, said a poem
begins in delight. He didn't mean a poem always begins in
merriment. He meant the joy of release or creativity, the kind
of delight we all feel at reading the kind of lines I've just quoted,
and the delight which must have filled James Shirley the 17th
century poet, when he found how to compress his thought into
images at once noble and concrete.

> The glories of our blood and state
> Are shadows, not substantial things
> There is no armour against fate.
> Death lays his icy hand on kings.
> Sceptre and crown
> Must tumble down
> And in the dust be equal made
> With the poor, crooked scythe and spade.

At last we've arrived at an example of true poetry, one which
answers our requirements and must stand for the moment for
the hundreds of others to be found.

(1969)

William Wordsworth

William Wordsworth had so much to say on the subject of poetry, and wrote so much poetry himself, that it's difficult to know where to begin talking about him. As a poet he produced an enormous amount of verse which some people still think to be generally excellent, but others regard as, in the main, repetitive and indifferent. As a critic of the art of poetry he shocked his contemporaries at first, but at last succeeded in convincing them. Perhaps the best way to begin is to talk about Wordsworth as a person and to let consideration of his theories and his verse arise as we go along.

William Wordsworth was born in the year 1770 in the town of Cockermouth, which is called the western gateway to the famous Lake District of England. As a child, or so he tells us himself, he was stiff and moody, with a violent temper: and his mother once said of him that of her five children, William was the one who was going to be remarkable, but whether for good or evil the poor woman couldn't venture a guess. His teachers probably held the same opinion, because if you ever have the chance to visit the school he attended in Hawkeshead you can still see that William spent at least one morning carving his name on the desk.

As well as his taste for woodcarving, he was fond of swimming, snaring, rock-climbing, bird-nesting, boat-stealing – all the things Old People have been deploring ever since Young People were first invented. He has written very honestly about these exploits in his long, autobiographical poem, *The Prelude*. He was sent to Cambridge in 1787 and in *The Prelude* has left us a very effective little snapshot of his lodging in St John's College.

> The Evangelist St John my patron was:
> Three Gothic courts are his, and in the first
> Was my abiding-place, a nook obscure;
> Right underneath, the College kitchens made
> A humming sound, less tuneable than bees,
> But hardly less industrious; with shrill notes
> Of sharp command and scolding intermixed.
> Near me hung Trinity's loquacious clock
> Who never let the quarters, night or day
> Slip by him unproclaimed, and told the hours
> Twice over with a male and female voice.
> Her pealing organ was my neighbour too;
> And from my pillow looking forth by light
> Of moon of favouring stars, I could behold
> The Ante-Chapel where the statue stood
> Of Newton, with his prism, and silent face
> The marble index of a mind forever
> Voyaging through strange seas of Thought,
>   alone.

During a holiday from Cambridge he set off on a walking tour of France and Switzerland and came back full of the new ideas about freedom and the equality of man which were setting the scene for the early stages of the French Revolution. Then, in 1798, he published *Lyrical Ballads*, a collection of poems which were the joint production of Wordsworth and his friend Coleridge. It contained twenty-two poems; the four by Coleridge included 'The Ancient Mariner', and there were eighteen by Wordsworth. In 1800 the second edition was published and for this Wordsworth wrote his famous *Preface* setting out his theories of the art of poetry.

The theories were such an attack on prevailing ideas of poetry and the nature of poetry that they enraged the critics;

and the poems were so simple that the reviewers ridiculed them. The argument went something like this: 'In the first place, Mr Wordsworth,' said the reviewers, 'there is no loftiness of expression in your poetry.'

And Wordsworth answered that one: 'What you really mean is that there is no poetic diction. I know there isn't. I *hate* poetic diction. I have consciously avoided it.'

And the reviewers said: 'But where are the figures of speech that are proper to poetry and that we have all a right to expect? Where are the personifications, where is the imagery. Where is beauty of expression?' Wordsworth replied:

> If a figure of speech is prompted by genuine passion – I use it. But I reject figures of speech when they are used as a mere mechanical device of style. I reject what you call beauty of expression, when what you really mean is a wellworn collection of bombastic and high flown inanities. I have even abstained from the use of expressions in themselves proper and beautiful, but which have been foolishly repeated by bad poets, till such feelings of disgust are connected with them as it is scarcely possible by any art of association to overpower.

So the reviewers had another look at the poems and complained (1) that the language was the language of prose and (2) that the subject matter was trivial and everyday, not at all dignified or elevated enough to be used for poetry, and (3) that instead of mythological personages with difficult names, or people of noble birth, or at least well-educated youths and cultivated maidens, the characters seemed to be all humble peasants without either position or property.

But Wordsworth in his Preface had already set out his answer to all these objections:

> My principle object in writing the poems was to choose incidents from common life and to describe them as far as possible in language really used by men – and at the same time to throw over them a certain colouring of

imagination, whereby these ordinary things would be presented to the mind in an unusual aspect. I chose humble and rural life because in that condition the passions of the heart are less under restraint and speak a plainer and more emphatic language.

But of course the reviewers couldn't accept this at all; it was too humble and common or garden altogether for the noble art of poetry. And they said they could see no merit whatever in Wordsworth's verse. Wordsworth's answer was: 'How could you? Those accustomed to the gaudiness and inane phraseology of so many modern writers are bound to be disappointed in my verse.'

As you can see, Wordsworth could wag as bitter a tongue as the next. But he could also do what many of his critics couldn't do: he could define what he meant by poetry: 'Poetry is Truth, carried alive into the heart by Passion.'

Today people accept that Wordworth's views were the right ones. But in his own times men's ideas about poetry had become confused by the very history of poetry itself. From the time of Chaucer, who can be said to represent the beginning of modern poetry, poets had been developing their art and discovering ways of expression, so that in different ages people expected different things from their poets. Chaucer wrote poetry about ordinary people which was simple and straightforward in its language and dealt for the most part with ordinary people and ordinary things. Wordsworth loved Chaucer and advised people to read him again and even modernised some of his *Tales* himself.

Then came Shakespeare, who made an orchestra of the English language, and then Milton, who used it more like a great organ:

> Captain or Colonel or Knight in Arms
> Whose chance on these defenceless doors may seize
> If deed of honour did thee ever please
> Guard them, and him within protect from harms.
> He can requite thee; for he knows the charms

That call fame on such gentle acts as these
And he can spread thy name o'er lands and seas
Whatever clime the sun's bright circle warms:
Lift not thy spear against the muses bower
The great Emathian conqueror did spare
The house of Pindarus, when temple and tower
Went to the ground: and the repeated air
Of sad Electra's poet had the power
To save the Athenian walls from ruin bare.

Wordsworth liked Milton too, though with all the classical illusions and so on I sometimes wonder why.

However, with Milton the line of poets of mighty imagination and exquisite fancy came to an end. Starting with Dryden, and developing through Pope and the Augustan poets, wit, philosophy, learning, took their place. Poets wrote a new kind of verse, mostly in heroic couplets, in which they were either insufferably learned and pompous and dealt at length with philosophical or classical themes; or sprightly and witty and concerned to comment on men and manners in an artificial state of society. I said that Shakespeare's language had the sweep of an orchestra and Milton's the grandeur of an organ. After Milton poets, when they were good, made a rapier of the English language; and when they were bad, a bludgeon. Poetry was no longer aimed at the hearts of all men, but at the heads of a few: at philosophers, professors, politicians, wits, and people who regarded themselves as being uniquely blessed in the matters of fashion and good taste. Language became as artificial as society itself. No self-respecting poet would ever get caught in a storm – it had to be a tempest. If the day was warm and sunny he talked about Phoebus and his beams and, if a poet fell in love (which became an occupational hazard with poets, especially dull poets), it was all due to Cupid and his darts.

The truth is that poetry had retreated into the study, complete with a whole glossary of poetic expressions, figures of speech, high-flown phrases and the rest. It was too puffed up and self-important to mix with the people or be seen without its wig and walking stick. This process had begun away back with Milton who, T.S. Eliot said, despite his greatness, wrote English as if it were a dead language and it had its climax in Dr Johnson, who spoke it as though he'd been to school in Ancient Rome. Listen to him talking about the poet Gray's letters about travel. What Dr Johnson wants to say is, simply, that he wishes Gray could have spent more time travelling and writing about his travels. Here's how he puts it:

> He that reads Gray's epistolary narration wishes that to travel and to tell his travels had been more to his employment.

No wonder poor Goldsmith said that if Dr Johnson wrote a fable about little fishes that talked they'd all talk like whales.

Wordsworth disliked Dryden and Pope and couldn't bear Dr Johnson. He once took the opening couplet of Johnson's poem 'On The Vanity of Human Wishes' and used it as an example of the unmeaning verbiage of the poetry of the time:

> Let Observation with extensive view
> Survey mankind from China to Peru.

Wordsworth pointed out that the same idea is repeated three times. He paraphrased it in this way: 'Let Observation, with extensive observation, observe mankind.'

In fact, he said, if you took the first line away, the second line would convey all that needed to be conveyed: 'Observe mankind from China to Peru.'

When Dr Johnson died, Wordsworth was eighteen. He was determined, as a poet, to rescue poetry from the study and set it walking again in the streets and the fields: to save it from those who thought wisdom proceeded from learning and restore it to those who knew that true wisdom comes always from the heart. He said of his own poems: 'I have wished to keep the reader in the company of flesh and blood, persuaded that by so doing I shall interest him.'

How well he succeeded in doing so you can easily judge

by comparing, let us say, his 'The Solitary Reaper' with
Milton's 'L'Allegro'. Milton, you'd think, had never muddied
a shoe on a country road or torn his breeches trying to climb
over a gate. The language is magnificent, but those shepherds
and shepherdesses are like ornaments you'd see on a mantelpiece – no blood in them at all. Whereas Wordsworth's
Reaper is a girl who could sharpen a scythe and who has been
burnt by the sun. And the poet who listens to her has a heart
in his breast too, capable of being moved by the sorrows of
flesh and blood.

> Behold her, single in the field,
> Yon solitary Highland Lass!
> Reaping and singing by herself;
> Stop here, or gently pass!
> Alone she cuts and binds the grain,
> And sings a melancholy strain;
> O listen! for the Vale profound
> Is overflowing with the sound.
>
> No nightingale did ever chaunt
> More welcome notes to weary bands
> Of travellers in some shady haunt,
> Among Arabian sands:
> A voice so thrilling ne'er was heard
> In springtime from the cuckoo-bird
> Breaking the silence of the seas
> Among the farthest Hebrides.
>
> Will no one tell me what she sings?
> Perhaps the plaintive numbers flow
> For old, unhappy, far-off things,
> And battles long ago:
> Or is it some more humble lay,
> Familiar matter of today?
> Some natural sorrow, loss, or pain
> That has been, and may be again?
>
> Whate'er the theme, the maiden sang

> As if her song could have no ending;
> I saw her singing at her work,
> And o'er the sickle bending;
> I listened, motionless and still;
> And, as I mounted up the hill,
> The music in my heart I bore,
> Long after it was heard no more.

Wordsworth deliberately cut himself off from the rich diction, the surging rhythms, the noble embellishments of the Elizabethans. Equally he rejected the wit and grace and elegance of Pope and the dignified learning of Johnson. He sought lyricism, simple diction, spontaneity. He didn't always stick rigidly to his own theories, and sometimes when he did his verse becomes as a result bald and trivial. His longer poems, such as *The Prelude*, have excellent passages; yet taken as a whole they tend to reiterate the same sentiment until they become dull and weary to the reader. But he set poetry back again on the right path and he did so by steadfastly refusing to acknowledge any other source of truth and wisdom than that of simple people, nature, and the lovely solitudes of his beloved Lake Country. There he spent the greater part of his life, exploring with his sister Dorothy and his poet companions, or walking all alone in contemplation until Nature became for him not simply the magnificent handiwork of God, but something which for him seemed to have a separate being of itself. He expresses this almost mythical belief in Nature in his lines written above Tintern Abbey:

> I have learned
> To look on Nature, not as in the hour
> Of thoughtless youth: but hearing oftentimes
> The still, sad music of humanity,
> Not harsh nor grating, though of ample power
> To chasten and subdue. And I have felt
> A presence that disturbs me with the joy
> Of elevated thoughts; a sense sublime
> Of something far more deeply interfused

Whose dwelling is the light of setting suns
And the round ocean and the living air
And the blue sky and in the mind of man;
A motion and a spirit, that impels
All thinking things, all objects of all thought
And moves through all things.

That, I think, is Wordsworth at his greatest. Let me finish by quoting what his contemporary, the great critic Hazlitt, who didn't by any means accept all Wordsworth's theories, had to say of him during his lifetime:

> The daisy looks up to him with sparkling eye as an old acquaintance: the cuckoo haunts him with sounds of early youth: a linnet's nest startles him with boyish delight: an old, withered thorn is weighed down with a heap of recollections: a grey cloak, seen on some wild moor, torn by the wind or drenched in the rain, afterwards becomes an object of imagination to him: even the lichens on the rock have a life and being in his thoughts.

To him the meanest flower that blows can give
Thoughts that do often lie too deep for tears.

(1969)

On Being Ourselves

You may ask what I think is the hardest thing in life to be. To my mind, the hardest thing of all to be is to be yourself. In the writing of poetry, it is often extremely difficult to be yourself.

For example, think of what happens if you ask someone to write a poem. Nine times out of ten, instead of expressing something he has felt and experienced himself, he'll write about something someone else has written about, and he'll express exactly the same sentiments expressed by that somebody else. I bet he'll write about a nightingale, or a skylark, or a daisy, or something religious, or something patriotic. He'll write:

> Ah, Skylark, when I hear thee sing
> What rapture it to me doth bring.

Some of the people who write like that wouldn't know the difference between a skylark's song and a referee's whistle, but they do it because skylarks have a habit of cropping up in poetry and they feel that that's the sort of sentiment skylarks have every right to expect from would-be poets. It's very hard not to imitate others, not to think as others do, not to say what others have said hundreds of times before. It's very hard to be original. Yet, when it comes to poetry, originality is a first necessity. And originality is not turning everything upside down and inside out, but finding how to define our own unique experiences and to express them in language we have made our own. To be original, we must learn to be ourselves.

That's why poetry changes from age to age. Wordsworth found a whole generation of bad poets using secondhand images and worn-out forms instead of struggling to find forms to suit themselves. His reaction was to throw all their high falutin' language and classical images and artificial emotions out the window.

When T.S. Eliot and the post-World War One poets came on the scene, they too had to reject the tradition of the poets who had preceded them – the Georgian poets. When T.S. Eliot, for example, wanted to express the mood and passions of that post-war age, the sentiments of the Georgians wouldn't do at all. This is not to say that the Georgian school didn't have good poets. It had excellent poets, of noble and valid sentiment, who wrote with a fine feeling for language. Although they used conventional forms derived mostly from Byron and Tennyson and Browning, most of them wrote like poets.

In his poem 'The Soldier', Rupert Brooke, one of the best of the Georgian poets, reveals the gentleness and the capacity for nobility and self-sacrifice which were characteristic of the young men of his generation:

> If I should die, think only this of me;
> That there's some corner of a foreign field
> That is for ever England. There shall be
> In that rich earth a richer dust concealed;
> A dust whom England bore, shaped, made aware.
> Gave, once, her flowers to love, her ways to roam,
> A body of England's, breathing English air,
> Washed by the rivers, blest by suns of home.

But when T.S. Eliot came to write, man's mood had changed. The romantic view of life had gone; the view of war and patriotism as a noble thing had vanished – it had died in the mud and blood and suffering of Flanders, where men met death not like warriors with swords and shining armour, but like sheep in a slaughterhouse or rats in a multitude of shell holes. There was heroism, certainly, but it was not the heroism of rhetoric. It was the resigned, tight-lipped heroism of men who knew they were being murdered for the insanity of kings and emperors, which is what Siegfried Sassoon says in his poem, 'On Passing the New Menin Gate'. When the survivors returned to their homes all over Europe after the War, they faced years of hunger, mass unemployment and poverty. The Georgian poets had nothing to say about a situation like that; so T.S. Eliot went back to the Elizabethans with their sense of guilt and sin and death and in particular John Donne, who had struggled harder than most poets to find some answer to despair. Eliot has written in one of his poems:

> Webster was much possessed by death
> And saw the skull beneath the skin.

And so, indeed, was Eliot: much possessed by death, by man's dishonesty and cruelty, and neglect of the word of God. Here are his sentiments in 'The Rock'.

> The word of the Lord came unto me, saying
> O miserable cities of designing men,
> O wretched generation of enlightened men
> Betrayed in the mazes of your ingenuities,
> Sold by the proceeds of your proper inventions:
> I have given you hands which you turn from worship,
> I have given you speech, for endless palaver,
> I have given you my law, and you set up commissions,
> I have given you lips, to express friendly sentiments,
> I have given you hearts, for reciprocal distrust.
> I have given you the power of choice and you only
>   alternate
> Between futile speculation and unconsidered action.
> Many are engaged in writing books and printing them
> Many desire to see their names in print,
> Many read nothing but the race reports.
> Much is your reading, but not the word of God
> Much is your building, but not the House of God,

Will you build me a house of plaster, with corrugated
    roofing
To be filled with a litter of Sunday newspapers?

This is very different from Brooke. Eliot's bitterness and
despair at the materialism and selfishness of his age led him
to a new way of writing poetry that caused a great sensation
at first. Even when his disgust had softened a little, as it had
by the time he wrote 'Journey of the Magi', it is not the
romance or the colour of the event that engages him – the
star, the stable, the rich gifts and the important travellers
kneeling in the straw – but rather the dirt of the inns, the
greed of the inn-keepers, the desertion of the bearers, the
foreshadowing of the baby's betrayal, the three crosses of
Calvary, seen in those three trees on the skyline, and the
dividing of Christ's garments by lot. With Eliot, a new age
of poetry had begun – hard, highly critical of men and society,
unsentimental – which continued through such poets as
Auden and Spender.

While Eliot was re-fashioning English verse – and even
before him – another poet as great, if not indeed greater,
our own W.B. Yeats, was struggling with the same problem.
Eliot rejected the Georgians and found his own style in which
to be himself. Yeats did more. He rejected his own early poetry,
created a distinctively Irish kind of poetry and kept on
remaking himself as a poet in the process.

The hardest thing to be, I've said, is to be yourself. Bad
poets never find out who they are. They take their forms and
their ideas at second-hand, they express second-hand emotions,
they imitate others. Good poets struggle to find their real selves,
to express the unique truth that is in each and every one of
us by right of being born. The soul stores up its own memories
and impressions, of parents and grandparents, of places, of
tradition; it has a sense of the history (what critics call the
Identity) of its own people, and a sense of the past which
Wordsworth is referring to when he speaks of 'Old, unhappy,
far-off things, / And battles long ago'. This sense of one's own

truth, of one's own race, one's tradition, one's past, is part
of our true selves. To be yourself, you must know where you
belong. And when you try to express this self, through the
art of poetry, it is an enormous help to have a heritage of verse
forms and rhythms and images and so on which have been
discovered by great poets who have at least shared in your
birthright. Brooke, in the poem we quoted earlier, had a form
already made for him, and no doubt whatever about where
he belonged.

> There shall be
> In that rich earth a richer dust concealed:
> A dust whom England bore, shaped, made aware.
> Gave, once, her flowers to love, her ways to roam,
> A body of England's, breathing English air,
> Washed by the rivers, blest by suns of home.

Wordsworth, Brooke, Eliot, all had a heritage of verse to consult
which had been shaped to the needs of self-expression by poets
who were at least their fellow-countrymen, all drawing on a
store of common social and racial experience. Yeats had not.
Neither had Goldsmith nor Thomas Moore, nor any of the
Irish poets working in English verse. The poetry of both Moore
and Goldsmith, to take the two best known of them, suffered
as a result, Moore's quite disastrously. Hazlitt, the critic, put
his finger on this right away. Here is a criticism he offered
of Moore's verse during Moore's own lifetime.

> It has been too much our Author's object to pander to
> the artificial taste of the age, and his productions, however
> brilliant and agreeable, are in consequence somewhat
> meretricious and effeminate. Rather than have any lack
> of excitement, he repeats himself; and 'Eden' and 'bliss'
> and 'cherub-smiles' fill up the pauses of the sentiment
> with sickly regularity.

English society, however admirable, was no part of Moore's
true self. Its way of expression was not truly his, its sentiments
were not *his* sentiments, however much he tried to adopt

them as his own. In fact his best verse is written when he is trying to match his verse to the Irish metres which were sometimes imposed on him when he was fitting his words to the rhythms of Irish folk songs. Here is an example of one of these poems:

At the mid hour of night, when stars are weeping, I fly
To the lone vale we loved, when life shone warm in thine
     eye;
And I think oft, if spirits can steal from the regions of air
To revisit past scenes of delight, thou wilt come to me
     there,
And tell me our love is remembered, even in the sky.

The rhythm there is characteristic of Gaelic poetry like this. The strange thing is that Moore himself was unaware of the freshness these rhythms lent to his verse. He admired the conventional English rhythms and complained that in having to write to the airs, he was forced to adopt what he termed 'a lawless kind of metre'. Another Irish poet, Jeremiah Joseph Callanan, complained in more or less the same way. For years Callanan's models were English and his poetry was lifeless and uninteresting; and when he finally became a popular poet through his translations of Irish poetry into English, he felt he had to apologise for the vulgarity of these simple songs of the people. Yet Callanan, too, was gaining freshness from contact with the real life around him. Listen to this verse of his:

'Tis down by the lake where the wild tree fringes its sides
That the maid of my heart, my fair one of heaven abides.
I think as at even she wanders its mazes along
The birds go to sleep by the sweet, wild twist of her song.

This is the same rhythm as 'At the mid hour of night when stars are weeping, I fly. . . .' Both Callanan and Moore had a body of verse available to them in which sentiment and manner were in harmony with the passions they themselves had inherited, but they never realised it, and they made use of it only through the accident of translating old verse or setting words to old tunes.

What consistently prevents Moore from finding a true expression of himself is his imitation of a society which was not truly his own; what frequently saves him is a singular event of his youth: the profound effect on him of the execution of his friend Robert Emmet, and as a consequence, his identification of himself with Ireland and her tragedy.

The same thing applies to Goldsmith. Goldsmith followed the literary fashion of his time. He used the heroic couplet and tried to write in the manner of an age dominated by the erudite Dr Johnson. But he cherished in his heart memories of home and love of family, and he allowed these, or couldn't prevent them, from overflowing into his verse. But again, as in the case of Moore and Callanan, although he was a greater poet by far than either, his verse suffers because he is never certain whether he should be thinking in terms of an English or an Irish background. If you examine 'The Deserted Village', you'll find the village is neither English nor Irish, and that the characters have the same ambivalence. But the poem is great in spite of these things because Goldsmith was in deadly earnest. His earnestness grew out of his own nature, his warmth and tenderness of heart, his ready compassion and, when he was being himself, it gave profundity to his verse. He knew how to be himself for most of the time, very often in spite of himself! He used to give his money away to the destitute and the outcasts in so profligate a fashion that poor Dr Johnson, who loved him, had a terrible time trying to save Goldsmith from the baliffs and the debt collectors.

W.B. Yeats had the same growing pains, so to speak. He began by being influenced by such poets as Spenser and Shelley and in his early published work, by Rossetti – that is to say, by the fashion of a Victorian society far removed from the little world of Sligo which was the most real part of Yeats.

It was through meeting with the Fenian, John O'Leary, that Yeats came to realise that his material lay about him: in folk tales and songs, in legends and ancient custom, and in national thinking. He said so himself: 'From O'Leary's conversation and from the Irish books he lent me has come all I have set my hand to since.' O'Leary introduced him to the poets of the *Nation,* to Davis and Mangan and Ferguson, and although Yeats – and even O'Leary – recognised them as being not very great poets, nevertheless they supplied a tradition and a background, something to which to belong, that was much more fruitful for Yeats than Rossetti and the pre-Raphaelite poets of London. Yeats declared himself to be a follower of the Irish tradition:

> Know that I would accounted be
> True brother of a company
> That sang to sweeten Ireland's wrong
> Ballad and story, rann and song. . . .
> Nor may I less be counted one
> With Davis, Mangan, Ferguson
> Because to him who ponders well
> My rhymes more than their rhyming tell
> Of things discovered in the deep
> Where only body's laid asleep.

From the time of his meeting with O'Leary, Yeats worked hard to escape from his early style which was slow and ornate and elaborate, full of dimly seen people who are wrapped about in magical mists, and to write in everyday language of the life that went on about him. For a long time the old style clung to his work, even while Irish nationalism and folklore were providing most of his material. In the end, however, he abandoned these too and became largely an autobiographical poet so that to understand him properly we should learn something of his childhood in Sligo, his parents' families, his love for Maud Gonne, his patriotic activities, the Civil War, his work as a Senator in the newly-founded Free State and so on. His poem 'He Wishes for the Cloths of Heaven' is written in his pre-Raphaelite style.

> Had I the heavens' embroidered cloths,
> Enwrought with golden and silver light

The blue and the dim and the dark cloths
Of night and light and the half-light
I would spread the cloths under your feet:
But I, being poor, have only my dreams;
I have spread my dreams under your feet;
Tread softly because you tread on my dreams.

That's a good example of his early style: ornate, elaborate, very beautiful – but soft and effeminate. He cast it aside in favour of everyday language, because in the long run a coloured style was as useless to Yeats in his effort to express the tensions of his country and his age as were the nobility and rich language of the Georgians to Eliot. How much more straightforward and muscular is his 'Easter 1916':

I have met them at close of day
Coming with vivid faces,
From counter or desk among grey
Eighteenth century houses.
I have passed with a nod of the head
Or polite, meaningless words
Or have lingered a while and said
Polite, meaningless words,
And thought, before I had done
Of a mocking tale, or a gibe
To please a companion
Around the fire at the club,
Being certain that they and I
But lived where motley is worn:
All changed, changed utterly:
A terrible beauty is born.

There's hardly a poetic word in that, and yet it is individualistic, it has strength, and it's worth a whole shipload of ballads of Fr Gilligan, with their moth hours of eve and times of sparrow chirp.

Yeats worked his whole life at the effort to be himself, and in doing so he not only became a great poet but he solved the dilemma of earlier Irish poets which I referred to when speaking about Goldsmith and Moore and Callanan. He disposed of all their uncertainties and misgivings, he pointed back towards the Irish tradition of literature and poetry and drew it all together into the great body of his own work. When he died, Ireland had its own poetic heritage revealed to it; Irish poets of the future could no longer have doubts about where they belonged.

(1969)

The Parting Guest

Frank O'Connor once remarked that although we know relatively little about Shakespeare's personal life, we can get the meaning of his work and the measure of its greatness simply by reading it; whereas to understand and enjoy the full flavour of a writer such as Swift, for instance, it is necessary to know something more: something of his personal affairs, something of the politics of his times and the society he lived in, something of his friends and contemporaries. The reason – or at least one of the reasons – is that Shakespeare, and indeed the Elizabethans generally, for all the excitement of conquest and growing power, lived in a stable world which held a common view of the meaning and purpose of life. God was in heaven, the questions of who made man and what was he destined for had all been looked after. There were hints, of course, of more things in nature than were dreamt of in philosophy, and there were the beginnings of a new spiritual and intellectual ferment, but they troubled the individual heart only, not, as yet anyway, the heart of the age. The Elizabethan knew where he stood in relation to this life and had clear rules by which to assess his chances in the next. He had quarrels about how God should be worshipped, but not whether He existed. This certitude applied to the social order as well. The Elizabethan knew his place and degree. Rebellion against authority was a deadly sin; dissent was disturbing and therefore chastised. If the proposition that all men were equal had ever been put to Shakespeare, he'd have given it to the gatekeeper or the gravedigger as a funny line. Shakespeare, by and large, took things as he found them.

Swift didn't. He raged against the injustices of society, against hypocrisy, against the misuse of power, against the arrogance of fools and the infirmity of the flesh. He addressed a lot of his attention to what was directly under his nose, and for that reason we have to know something about that activity to fully appreciate him. He named names (as they say) and he had the modern conceit of the all-importance of the individual. Whatever Swift thought, felt or suffered was, in his view, worth writing about; and, naturally, worth reading about. So, once again, we have often to know the context to get the point.

I was set thinking about that distinction between Shakespeare and Swift by the three poems I wish to discuss here*: first because it seems to me to apply to Yeats as well – not the early Yeats perhaps – but to Yeats in his maturity; and the three poems are from his mature period. To be fully appreciated they demand information about the poet's life and thought that is not wholly present in the poems themselves. A second reason for thinking of it was that, at the time he wrote them, Yeats was looking back to the eighteenth century in Ireland as a period of unique intellectual enlightenment, and I believe his study of Swift in particular accounts for the spare and direct style in which they are written.

From 1922 to 1930 Yeats became bitterly disillusioned with the new Ireland, its hatreds, its obscurantism, its anti-artistic and anti-intellectual attitudes. The period from Swift through to Grattan seemed to offer better food for reflection and he felt closer to the spirit and thought of its great men – to Swift, Burke, Berkeley, Goldsmith – than he did to the largely parish pump debates of his own times. With Swift he identified particularly. He not only wrote a play about him and turned his epitaph into a poem; he refers frequently to him in his works, not simply as a writer long dead, but almost as a living

---

* 'Sailing to Byzantium', 'Among School Children and 'The Circus Animals' Desertion'.

contemporary. Yeats's thinking and manner of expression
during this period, his cynicism, his spareness, his rages, all
seem to have echoes of Swift. For instance, in 'Blood and the
Moon', in which he talks of the old Norman tower he had
restored to live in as an emblem of the poet's need for strength
and isolation and yet continuity of generation, he says:

> In mockery I have set
> A powerful emblem up
> And sing it rhyme upon rhyme
> In mockery of a time
> Half dead at the top

Now the time he mocks as being 'half dead at the top' is
Ireland of the period 1922 and into the thirties, and the
expression is an echo of a remark Swift once made when he
confessed to a friend his fear of going mad: 'Like an old tree
I shall die at the top.' Yeats goes on:

> I declare this tower is my symbol; I declare
> This winding, gyring, spiring, treadmill of a stair is my
>   ancestral stair;
> That Goldsmith and the Dean, Berkeley and Burke have
>   travelled there.
> Swift beating on his breast in sibylline frenzy blind
> Because the heart in his blood-sodden breast had dragged
>   him down to mankind,
> Goldsmith deliberately sipping at the honeypot of his
>   mind. . . .

The three poems, 'Sailing to Byzantium', 'Among School
Children' and 'The Circus Animals' Desertion' have this
Swiftian directness and clarity, something of his suppressed
rage too, and at the same time they have the poise of the
eighteenth century mind. They require, as I've said, some
knowledge of the poet's life and other works; and they were
written, I personally believe, in a conscious awareness on
Yeats's part of significant parallels between his own experiences
and those of Swift. We will go over Yeats's career to the extent

that it is relevant to an appreciation of the poems and refer incidentally to the Swiftian parallels that must have been in his thought, though not necessarily in the forefront of his thought.

As a young boy, he regarded poetry as a haven from the world of action. That was no mere prejudice of youth, or if it was, it never left him, for although he became a man of action for periods and a very formidable one (he started so many different movements Sean O'Casey once nicknamed him 'The great Founder') he was torn always between action and contemplation. His early style was slow and ornate and elaborate and when you read it, the poems, instead of settling into your head, seem to drift around you and brush past you like a dim vapour. To understand them you need to know nothing about the poet personally. He began 'The Wanderings of Oisin' around 1886, under the influence of John O'Leary, the Fenian, and became interested in nationalism. He also became interested in magic and the occult. In 1889, the year 'The Wanderings of Oisin' was published, he met Maud Gonne, who was celebrated for her beauty. Yeats was twenty four at the time and fell deeply in love with her. She had strong nationalistic feelings too, and for her sake Yeats increased his own involvement. He wrote the play *The Countess Cathleen,* and founded a national theatre movement, as part of a plan to satisfy her desire to awaken feelings of Irish nationality. Later he wrote *Cathleen Ni Houlihan* for her to act in. He regarded her at that stage as an Irish Joan of Arc, though later her political involvement irked him.

His relationship with her was a strange one. He worshipped her without reservation and yet she was timid of the normal physical expressions of love. He wished to marry her, but she evaded the matter while leaving him with the impression that there was still hope. At last, after some years of uncertainty and agony, Yeats succumbed to the advances of another woman who was in love with him, but abandoned the affair and again returned to his absorption with Maud Gonne. Swift had a similar relationship with Stella and was pursued by Vanessa until he violently rejected her. Swift had also taken up national causes and was at one time actively involved in politics as Yeats was to become later, when he was appointed a Senator of State.

Side by side with his passion for Maud Gonne and his work for the theatre and the national cause, he continued to explore the occult as a Theosophist and later as a member of a society founded by Madame Blavatsky and called – rather impressively – The Hermetic Students of the Golden Dawn. Yeats regarded the artist as a type of magician, capable of extrasensory perception, whose craft it was to unravel mysteries and discover truths through the interpretation of dreams and the discovery of key symbols. He sought what he himself termed 'The Eternal Rose of Beauty and Peace', a sort of Beatific vision granted to initiates who had established contact with the world of the Gods. Yeats, at that stage of his development, although he took part in a great deal of practical activity, couldn't bear too much reality. The dreamer in him, the timid and retiring part of his nature, prefered the shadowy and narcotic regions of the half-world.

His affair with Maud Gonne came to a dramatic end in 1903. He was getting ready to give a lecture one night when a letter from Maud Gonne was handed to him. It told him she had just married Major John McBride in Paris. He carried on with his lecture but never afterwards could he remember a word he had said.

If he lost Maud Gonne finally that night, he gained something of importance to his art: the determination to find a new style. The early Yeats was a minor poet and possibly would have remained one. That night in 1903 the world changed its meaning for him. The old romanticism was now irrelevant. High sentence and histrionics had no meaning any longer. To face the world with dignity and to hold his very being together it was necessary to wear a mask, for a mask conceals the hurt and suffering deep in the heart. From then on, Yeats's attitudes and methods begin to change. In fact he tells of that change in a poem.

All things can tempt me from this craft of verse;
One time it was a woman's face, or worse
The seeming needs of my fool driven land.
Now nothing but comes readier to the hand
Than this accustomed toil. When I was young
I had not given a penny for a song
Did not the poet sing it with such airs
That one believed he had a sword upstairs;
Yet would be now, could I but have my wish
Colder and dumber and deafer than a fish.

No more stilted boys and romantic notions. A new way of seeing and a new way of saying had to be found. And while he was still striving for that detachment, that 'Unity of Being' as he himself called it, the Hermetic Students of the Golden Dawn, although his absorption with them had provided him with symbols for his art which he would still make use of from time to time, began to recede in importance too. In 1915, at the age of 50, he wrote that the leopards of the moon, the wild witches, the holy centaurs of the hills, had all vanished, and he ended with the line: 'I must endure the timid sun.'

Meanwhile, the Rising of 1916 had provided another unexpected jolt. He had regarded the prelude to it as so much play-acting and bravado, but the Rising and the executions showed how wrong his assessment had been. By an irony of fate, the man who had married Maud Gonne and whom Yeats once described as 'a drunken, vainglorious lout', Major John McBride, was one of the executed leaders.

With the setting up of the new State Yeats became a Senator. Then came the disillionment of Civil War and after it a society which seemed to him anti-intellectual and dull and bourgeois, concerned at best with the merely sensual and at worst with the material and the unimaginative.

By 1925, when he wrote 'Sailing to Byzantium' and 'Among School Children', all these things were behind him. He had found and mastered his new style, he had been honoured by the State, he had been awarded the Nobel prize. Yet there was

no solution to his personal unease in the accumulation either
of honours or of experience. 'My life,' he once said, 'seems
to me a preparation for what never happens.' Meanwhile, he
was sixty years of age: an old man. He had been conscious
of ageing and when he was describing his Nobel prize medal
he said this: 'It shows a young man listening to a muse, who
stands young and beautiful . . . and I think: I was good-looking
once, and now I am old and rheumatic. But my muse is young.'

These are things worth bearing in mind, together with the
fact that in 1926 he became so ill he very nearly died, when
we are reading the two poems I have mentioned, because they
are all part of the tensions and pre-occupations that had to
be beaten into a pulp before Yeats could bring them into unity
inside himself and make of them workable material for his art.
They account for the undercurrent of contradictory emotions
in the poems, the resignation and yet the agony of unrest and
they throw light on his methods. These are the poems of an
ageing man, looking back over a rich and dedicated life and
deliberately distilling the essence of his experiences into poems
which are as chiselled and hard as sculptures. Yeats's intention
was to purify and crystallise those experiences, to fix them and
give them permanence by sheathing them in a form and style
strong enough to withstand the shock of time. He must fix
them in his mind and in the mind of Time. Otherwise their
reality would be destroyed. For he wrote elsewhere that:

> (And) God-appointed Berkeley (that) proved all things
>   a dream,
> That this pragmatical, preposterous pig of a world, its
>   farrow that so solid seem,
> Must vanish on the instant if the mind but change its
>   theme.

Through poetry, Yeats strove to hold his world and being intact.
State honours, Nobel prizes, these were accidents that did no
more than amuse him. He summed up his attitude to them
in an epigram:

> Much did I rage when young
> Being by the world oppressed
> But now with flattering tongue
> It speeds the parting guest.

For him, Thought and Art were the important things, to be made durable through poetry:

> An agèd man is but a paltry thing
> A tattered coat upon a stick, unless
> Soul clap its hands and sing, and louder sing
> For every tatter in its mortal dress.

In Ireland there was no longer regard for poetry – no singing school, as he puts it – but a new nation engrossed only in images of its own importance – monuments of its own magnificence. So Yeats dismissed everyday life and substituted Byzantium, the centre of an old civilisation long vanished from the earth, but which still exists in the memory, where it is better than the reality, because imagination has perfected it and made it unchangeable. Yeats made Byzantium exist here and now; just as he made Swift and Burke exist here and now; through his art and intellect he was able to live in a fusing of two golden ages.

In that Byzantium which imagination has perfected and made permanent, everything lives in its own right; the mosaics have acquired life and awareness and have taken on personality. God's fire of creation and holiness animates them. They can subsume Yeats into their own eternity of perfect being, which is the resolution of self. I have heard it asked if, in the last stanza, Yeats really wishes to be transformed into a mosaic or an artificial singing bird. The answer I would give is 'no', if you are thinking of these things as inanimate, as artefacts. What Yeats desires is the consciousness of perfection and permanence which these images have the power to evoke in him. They transport him outside of time and, incidentally, release him from the decrepitude of age.

He has said elsewhere that whatever the passions of men

have gathered about, whatever men have venerated or contemplated deeply or honoured, become symbols in man's universal memory, capable of calling up angels or devils. He dwells on this power of images in the next poem, 'Among School Children', distinguishing between the statues and pictures which assist the nun in her devotions and arouse holy thoughts and the inward image of her son which a mother contemplates and finds solace in. Is it a physical image: of her son as a baby, as a boy, as a mature man? It's no one of these, but a non-visual thing – the essence behind the image, – which she has distilled out of love and her maternity, just as Yeats distils poems out of a multitude of experiences. In this poem too, we are back to memories of Maud Gonne, back to his preoccupation with the legend of Leda and the swan, his reading of the philosophers. I suggest the chief thought in it is this search for the essence. What is it that creates the unity which is his concept of the chestnut tree; of the act of dance and dancer; of Maud Gonne the child, the beautiful girl, the ageing woman; of the external image and the internal one? That is what Yeats searches for.

The undercurrent of anguish in the poems comes, I think, not wholly from resentment and impatience with old age, but because age is bringing Yeats's search for truth to an end before he has found it and because it is slowing down his ability to work at a moment when his creative excitement is unabated:

> What shall I do with this absurdity –
> O heart, O troubled heart – this caricature,
> Decrepit age that has been tied to me
> As to a dog's tail?
> Never had I more
> Excited, passionate, fantastical
> Imagination, nor an ear or eye
> That more expected the impossible

T.S. Eliot put the same complaint in another way when he wrote, in *The Four Quartets*:

What is the late November doing
With the disturbance of the Spring

Yeats called his ultimate goal 'Unity of Being', Eliot called it simply 'Home'. Again, Eliot talks of learning to master words in order to express something, only to find that that is no longer what he wants to express. His concept of truth keeps moving ahead of his technique. But, he decides, you must still explore:

Old men ought to be explorers
Here and there does not matter
We must be still – and still moving
Into another intensity
For a further union, a deeper communion
Through the dark cold and the empty desolation,
The wave cry, the wind cry, the vast waters
Of the petrel and the porpoise. In my end is my
  beginning.

For Yeats the end was a gathering together of the fragments as in 'The Circus Animals' Desertion', and the conclusion that man must live within the limitation of his human condition. A month or so before he died he acknowledged that whatever the soul's intimations, human understanding is limited, and he wrote it to a friend when he said: 'Man can embody truth, but he cannot know it. I must embody it in the completion of my life'.

Yeats created great poetry and yet in the end, as he recognised, he had found no ultimate answer, no 'Unity of Being' that could ever satisfy his restless pursuit of knowledge and perfection. In 'The Circus Animals' Desertion' he summed up his themes. Here's how he summed up his whole life:

What Then?
His chosen comrades thought at school
He must grow a famous man;
He thought the same and lived by rule,
All his twenties crammed with toil;
'What then?' sang Plato's ghost. 'What then?'

Everything he wrote was read,
After certain years he won
Sufficient money for his need,
Friends that have been friends indeed;
'What then?' sang Plato's ghost. 'What then?'

All his happier dreams came true –
A small old house, wife, daughter, son,
Grounds where plum and cabbage grew,
Poets and Wits about him drew;
'What then?' sang Plato's ghost. 'What then?'

'The work is done' grown old, he thought,
'According to my boyish plan;
Let the fools rage, I swerved in naught,
Something to perfection brought;'
But louder sang the ghost, 'What then?'

(1971)

It's No Go, My Honey Love

Sometime in 1943, when the war was biting very hard indeed and Ireland was clinging on by its fingertips to neutrality in the face of much fist-shaking from Britain and the US, Sean Lemass summed up the position for us simply and typically: 'Our main task is to stay alive,' he told us 'in a world where we have few friends.'

I am put in mind of his words by the characters discussed by Anthony Cronin in *Dead As Doornails*. To a greater or lesser extent they faced such a situation, though for them it outlived the war and persisted more or less as a permanent condition, a common fate. Indeed Cronin lays much of the blame on the war years, whether in Ireland or England: 'The creative and personal lives of nearly all the figures in this chronicle were more deeply affected and distorted by the war than may be immediately apparent.'

There are seven such characters, all now dead: Ralph Cusack, Patrick Kavanagh, Brendan Behan, Myles na Gopaleen, Robert MacBryde, Robert Colquhoun and Julian Maclaren Ross. Four of them I knew personally (it would have been something of a feat not to and yet be part of the Dublin scene in those years) though, with the possible exception of Ralph Cusack, not at all as intimately as did Anthony Cronin. Nevertheless I walked the self-same streets, attended Peadar O'Donnell's regular coffee sessions in Bewley's of Westmoreland Street, climbed the stairs to the cramped offices of *The Bell* in Lower

O'Connell Street and occasionally (I preferred other haunts) took my share of drink and abuse in McDaids of Harry Street.

There was a lot of abuse handed out in those days, I remember, all free, gratis and for nothing, though what it was about was, often enough, hard to work out. Some of it was merely the spin-off, I suppose, from people thrashing around, as Cronin puts it 'among yearnings, enthusiasms and despairs'. That the recipient might have similar afflictions was hardly ever understood.

Common to all seven characters was a drink problem which ranged from the severe to the ultimately self-destructive and in *Dead As Doornails* we are obliged, of necessity, to watch in each a decline in which creative expression either suffered neglect or became at last impossible. That is not at all to say that alcohol was the only villain of the piece, or even the principal one, or that it was of equal importance in all cases, but it played a large part. With Brendan Behan, Cronin believes, the matter was clinched when he appeared '. . . drunk on television with Malcolm Muggeridge and, in a sense beyond jest, his doom was accomplished.'

Perhaps so. Certainly his pursuit of a public image seemed to become reinforced thereafter by an irresistible inner urge to self-destruction. It was sad. Brendan before his decline was the best of company. And, as I have cause to know, generous in his estimate of his fellow writers. Cronin describes him happily in those early days: 'He was fat, it is true, for his height and age, but his girth combined with his personality gave the impression that he was somehow merely bursting at the seams.'

Myles na Gopaleen, of course, suffered cruelly when *At Swim-Two-Birds*, published in 1939, lost its proper hearing due to the outbreak of war. It is also said that *The Third Policeman* was rejected sometime around 1940 due to editorial changes and the war situation. The manuscript then mysteriously disappeared and was published only in 1965, when Myles was already dead.

Recognition of Paddy Kavanagh suffered equally from our war-time isolation and the incestuous situation here through the thirties and forties. Cronin's associate editorship of *The Bell* in the fifties provided the push (and the £5 per poem) which sustained a creative upsurge and produced most of the poems published later in *Come Dance with Kitty Stobling*. About that time too, John Ryan's *Envoy* offered him a platform and what I think is now called 'regular exposure'. But by then cancer and drink were combining to bring the play to an end.

Ralph Cusack lived to achieve *Cadenza,* a sort of autobiographical fantasy in a typically individualistic mode. He was also the author of a bulb catalogue which won the unusual distinction of being reviewed in the literary pages. Shortly after, however, ill-health and early excess put an end to it in the South of France where he had gone to live.

Robert MacBryde and Robert Colquhoun were painters whose success in London in the forties had become old hat there in the fifties. And Julian Maclaren Ross was also highly regarded there in the heyday of Penguin *New Writing* and *Horizon* but joined the neglected in his turn and became 'one of the ruined men of the forties'.

Ruin, indeed, is the ground bass of this book. And on a grand scale so repeated that it wears the face of inevitability. The eye Cronin casts on these lives is not quite a cold one, but it is unsentimental and penetrating. What it discerns is ultimately terrifying and so, arguably, true. He faces the facts squarely. What, then, prompted him to do so? The urge, no doubt, to chronicle a distinctive and largely tragic era in the history of Dublin's literary goings-on, which he captures vividly and nicely assesses. More personally, perhaps, it is his attempt at something which, though it may occupy a lifetime, can never quite succeed: the exorcism of ghosts.

(1976)

The Inferior Appetites

At the end of 1898, when W.B. Yeats and Edward Martyn called on George Moore in London to ask him to return to Dublin to help them set up a Literary Theatre, he was, as usual, sceptical.

'Giving a Literary Theatre to Dublin can't be serious,' he told them, 'it's like giving a mule a holiday.'

Moore's curiosity was always greater than his judgement and he came back, yet growing up thirty or forty years later in that same city one could well have wondered had it been worth his while. True, in the streets about our homes and schools the ghosts of that past, of Moore himself and Synge and Joyce and AE still lurked (indeed Yeats and Edward Martyn and Lady Gregory were still occasionally to be observed in the flesh); and the shouts and scuffles that had marked the first productions of *The Playboy of the Western World* and *The Plough and the Stars* were vibrations quivering in the air about us. But we were not encouraged to notice and we were unable – naturally – to guess. Literature – or most of it – was suspect. Belvedere preferred not to talk about its one-time pupil, James Joyce; Synge Street, though in no way responsible, took care to ignore the proximity of Bernard Shaw's birthplace. In a city that had become slightly deranged by literature and literary prejudice, it was almost impossible to discover what might be the purpose of literature and where it could be found. The quest, a personal one, for some understanding of the matter was obstructed – occasionally in a well-intentioned way – by Church, State, Nationalism, Patriotism, Puritanism and even remotely related notions of Self-Sufficiency.

But then literature, at the best of times, is a difficult thing to define and literary tastes are compounded, often enough, of sheer prejudice. Even Sean O'Casey, that least pretentious of men, never fully recovered from the shock of discovering that his paragon of high-mindedness, W.B. Yeats, read detective stories for relaxation. The State in those days had its own views on literature too. There was a Minister of State, a politician of unusual intellect, capable of producing a thesis on Statecraft based on his study of Thomistic philosophy who, whenever he travelled by tram, was repelled by the sight of the lumpen proletariat with their uncouth noses dug into the popular novels they had borrowed from the public libraries. To give him his due, his complaint was not so much their addiction to the stuff, but that they were indulging a low appetite at the expense of the taxpayer. He believed, in Thomistic fashion, that the inferior appetites are subordinate both to the good of the totality of man's being and to the welfare of the State; they were subordinate, therefore, to social justice and the common good.

When I myself was growing up, statesmen with educational advantages were inclined to theorise in that style. It was tedious, but at least they were a cut above the other kind, who managed to get through their political careers without any hint of a visitation from any abstraction whatever. Ministers also understood the functions of the State to include the privilege of deciding what the ordinary five-eighth should – or rather, should not – read. The outcome was State censorship and a wholesale banning of publications. This was latched on to with enormous zest by the Holy Willies. Their favourite hunting grounds were the shelves of the public libraries. They were determined to scour them clean of any hint of sin or obscenity. If the librarian was lax about removing offending material they did it for him, either by scoring over certain passages with pen or pencil, or by tearing out the offending pages altogether. Cardinal Newman's dictum, that in a sinful society you can't have a sinless literature, was not for them. Relics of that mad campaign turn up occasionally even still. It all took place long before the paperback revolution and long before the cheap editions were cheap enough to stock the shelves of a working-class household. It certainly made the search for some idea of what literature was all about a good deal more difficult than it ought to have been.

These were inauspicious beginnings to a personal search which was not helped by my own notions of the nature and purpose of literature: grandiose notions and dedicated ones, but simple-minded in the extreme. I believed as to means, that the longer the words the greater must be the writing; and that the function of literature was nothing less than to encompass a total wisdom which would unravel the mysteries of God, of Life and of the Universe. Like most adolescents, when they become aware of the eternal conundrum for the first time, I was a bit lost in the immensity of everything, and much depressed by the passing of time and the certainty of my own annihilation, and I was misled, I suppose, by all those wise looking statues of great writers and philosophers of the past into thinking they had succeeded in working out the answers. It took me a long time to discover they had not; that the dullest of them simply hammered out variations, however impressively, on the usual conventional and not very convincing explanations, while the best did no more than repeat the questions. I remember searching through the secondhand barrows on the quays, where you could pick up the life work of the Famous and the Forgotten for as little as tuppence or thrupence a volume, and finding most of them simply unreadable. Whatever world they had lived in (if they had lived in any at all, which I sometimes doubted) it had nothing to do with mine. Pope's summary of the secondhand barrows of eighteenth century London still held good for Dublin:

> Scotists and Thomists now in peace remain
> Amidst their kindred cobwebs in Duck-lane.

There were, of course, glowing exceptions, such as Swift

or Voltaire or Anatole France. They answered none of the eternal questions, but at least they had the grace to be witty, and sometimes savage, about the inescapable dilemma. They had brushed hard against the world and its realities, and they made you laugh about it, not just in your belly, but with your whole being. Laughter was one part of the answer; but no one can keep on laughing for further orders. Man, at the best of times, is a melancholy kind of animal. If he had literary leanings in Dublin in the late thirties, Authority with the connivance of conventional society had determined to depress him for life by banning most of his native writers and the best of those in the world beyond. A dense fog of obscurantism had settled, immovably it seemed, over the whole of Irish life.

Yet the odd book escaped, one of them being the *Canterbury Tales,* possibly because of its venerability. I began to read it around that time. I was still searching for explanations of the eternal perplexities and still hoping that at least one of the ancients and immortals would redeem their reputation as enlighteners. The fourteenth-century English, of course, was a difficulty, but it had an attraction of its own. If there really *was* such a thing as transcendental enlightenment, what was it more likely to be couched in than archaic language? And that made the struggle with Chaucer's medieval English worth a trial.

For pages and pages it rolled over my head and past my ears, an unfamiliar music that grabbed the attention and yet meant nothing at all. Then little by little the mists thinned out, the shapes slowly materialised, light flooded over the landscape. There was no trace of answers, explanations, solutions, no hint of the kind of enlightenment I'd been expecting. Instead there were people, very ordinary people, all on pilgrimage together:

> The holy blissful martir for to seeke
> That them hath holpen when that they were seeke.

It was a mixed company of nine and twenty mortals who were shortening the long journey to the Saint's resting place by telling a story, each in turn.

This was as near as I've ever got to the nature of literature in relation to life: an image of mankind journeying hopefully to a grave, leaving eternal truths to look after themselves, content with tales that knit them into a listening brotherhood simply by reflecting the dilemma that is the human condition. For that is what Chaucer dealt with, the human condition, and his characters – the gentle knight, the worldly monk, the rosy-cheeked nun, the drunken miller and the rest – all of them part of a world that had died five hundred years before, might still walk the streets and in their nature and their inmost preoccupations be indistinguishable from the rest of us.

I found that literature is a mirror into which a man looks, not for an answer or an explanation, but for the validity and faithfulness of the image. He sees himself there and he sees his neighbours and the world, and he says to himself (as Sean O'Faolain once expressed it to me): 'Yes, there we are – the whole ragbagful . . . That's exactly how we look; that's precisely how we are.'

And he does so with inexplicable satisfaction and an extraordinary sense of release. Why? My own explanation, which may satisfy nobody except myself, is that in reflecting ourselves and our neighbours and the world we live in, and in doing so with validity and faithfulness, literature pins it all down for our consideration and absorption.

It is a process which Authority here in the thirties and the forties tried desperately to prevent, a process which brings life, which is constantly hurrying and changing, constantly confusing and contradictory, into a condition of permanence and repose. Humanity sits still long enough to give a steady look at it. The glimpse it affords us doesn't necessarily edify us, nor does it resolve the ultimate mystery, but it assures us of plenty of company, all more or less equally mystified. It affirms a common humanity and experience, a general vulnerability, a shared loneliness, a sort of cosmic kinship. It records the bouts of laughter at little or nothing, the unspectacular virtues, the petty villainies. Literature is a celebration of the inferior appetites.

(1980)

From Hero to Artist

If the literary luminaries of Dublin around the turn of the century had anything in common (and they had a great deal – for all their squabbling) it was their habit of traipsing its streets at odd hours of the day and night, usually, it would seem, quite aimlessly. Yeats, for instance, was well known to the police for talking publicly with his muse and stepping unheeding under the hooves of passing horses. George Moore wandered regularly with his cousin Edward Martyn, although neither one could stand the other. AE cultivated the company of the younger men, such as Colum or Stephens. John Synge walked with Molly Allgood, although usually in the surrounding countryside, and usually discussing more intimate subjects than his latest poem or play. Oliver St John Gogarty and James Joyce were, for a time, inseparable. As were Joyce and his brother Stanislaus. I remark on the fact because the habit of both solitary and companionable peregrination is reflected throughout Joyce's work, one example being the passage about him setting out to attend college lectures in the morning from *A Portrait of the Artist as a Young Man*:

> The rainladen trees of the avenue evoked in him, as always, memories of the girls and women in the plays of Gerhart Hauptmann; and the memory of their pale sorrows and the fragrance falling from the wet branches mingled in a mood of quiet joy. His morning walk across

the city had begun, and he foreknew that as he passed
the sloblands of Fairview he would think of the cloistral,
silverveined prose of Newman; that as he walked along
the North Strand Road, glancing idly at the windows
of the provision shops, he would recall the dark humour
of *Guido Cavalcanti* and smile; that as he went by Baird's
stonecutting works in Talbot Place the spirit of Ibsen
would blow through him like a keen wind, a spirit of
wayward boyish beauty; and that passing a grimy marine
dealer's shop beyond the Liffey he would repeat the song
by Ben Jonson which begins:

    I was not wearier where I lay.

His brother Stanislaus has remarked that in early youth
James had been in love with vast conceptions and had believed
in the supreme importance of the world of ideas. The truth
of that can be seen in his early novel, *Stephen Hero*. But then,
Stanislaus goes on, the minute life of earth claimed him. In
the passage I've just quoted from *A Portrait of the Artist* one can
see the two views blending and becoming compatible. In it
Joyce is not only reflecting on the shadowy intimations of
international literature, he is keeping a sharp eye on the
realities of the passing scene: the stonecutter's yard, the marine
dealer's shop.

It was a world which belonged to his student days at the
National University which lasted from 1898 to 1902 and one
which was busying itself, as he thought, about all the wrong
things. Its Irish brand of Catholicism he found spiritually
unadventurous, obscurantist, arrogant and authoritarian. He
saw nationalism for the most part as mere bellicose posturing
and believed it to be firmly spancelled by the power of the
clergy. In *Stephen Hero*, when Madden is urging nationalistic
views on Stephen, Joyce says of Stephen:

The liberation which would have satisfied Madden would
by no means have satisfied *him*. The Roman, not the
Sassenach, was for him the tyrant of the islanders: and
so deeply had the tyranny eaten into all souls that the

intelligence, first overborne so arrogantly, was now eager
to prove that arrogance its friend.

Later in a much quoted Broadside he said the same thing
more pithily:

> O Ireland my first and only love
> Where Christ and Caesar are hand in glove.

The Literary Revival and its leading figures roused his scorn
and left him equally unimpressed. He saw it as looking back-
wards in romantic admiration at a peasant order which
disregarded intellect and was ruled by superstition. This led
him, among other targets, to attack Lady Gregory's *Poets and
Dreamers* in a review in the *Daily Express*, an uncompromising
stand from a never very grateful young man – Lady Gregory
had got him the job in the first place. Her book, he wrote,
'sets forth in the fulness of its senility a class of mind which
Mr Yeats has set forth with such delicate scepticism in his
happiest book: *The Celtic Twilight.*'
Elsewhere, in reviewing the collected verse of a much
esteemed patriotic poet recently dead, he wrote:

> [This verse] was written, it seems, for papers and societies
> week after week, and bears witness to some desperate
> and weary energy [while] . . . speaking of redemption
> and revenge, blaspheming against tyrants, and going
> forth full of tears and curses, upon its infernal labours.

Much of this, of course, is the disdain of an arrogant and
pugnacious young man, not far at times from going forth
himself full of curses, if not of tears. There was, nevertheless,
a reasonable measure of justification for it in the excesses of
the prevailing patriotism and myth-worship which had roused
his ire.
The Irish Literary Theatre was taken to task in much the
same spirit. In 'The Day of the Rabblement', which he
published in 1901, he attacked Yeats and Moore and Martyn
for sacrificing intellectual freedom in the cause of popular

nationalism, a strange charge to lay at the door of either Yeats or Moore; and went on to warn them that no man can be a lover of the true or the good unless he abhors the multitude. Neither Martyn nor Moore, he decided, were writers of much originality: Moore outdated, a man struggling in the backwash of literary history; Martyn 'disabled' (as he put it) by an incorrigible style. Such attacks on the sacred cows of the era – on religion, on nationalism, the Gaelic League, the literary movement and the new theatre movement – attracted considerable notice.

But perhaps what drew the most attention to him during his student period was the publication of his essay on Henrik Ibsen in April 1900 in *The Fortnightly Review* (the most important literary review in England), when he was as yet only eighteen years of age. Although Ibsen had transformed the stage in a world of theatre that had been existing on a diet of French farce, Dublin had known little or nothing about him. (Joyce's father, it seems, when he saw the play *Ghosts* lying about the home, thought it was a book about a haunted house). Joyce was greatly impressed by the technical dexterity and the clarity of perception in Ibsen's work; and by the nobility of a man whose soul sought for the stars, and whose unswerving determination was to be steadfast to his own self. 'I have a horror of the masses,' Ibsen had said. Joyce echoed the sentiment without reservation and flung it at real and imaginary enemies alike, sometimes with unbecoming intensity, as in a passage in *Stephen Hero* where he speaks of himself flinging disdain at them 'from flashing Antlers'.

These were the more public manifestations of Joyce the social and literary critic, the young man who sought intellectual order as the key to self-fulfilment. But there was also the more private search, the search for creative expression, and for that harmony which he believed *must* be found between inner and outer reality. His first attempt at literary form seems to have been a poem on the death of Parnell which he wrote at the age of nine or so and which his admiring father, a fanatical Parnellite, had printed for distribution to his friends. He also attempted a novel as co-author with a school friend around the age of ten. Somewhat nearer the mark he had written, again while still at school, some stories which he called silhouettes. According to Stanislaus, they were in the style of *Dubliners*. He also wrote a play, called *A Brilliant Career*, which he showed to William Archer and later burned. But it was while he was at university, it seems, that he began his more serious work, experimenting with poetry and writing minor lyrics which combined melody and grace in an archaic mode. He also began to record experiences which he called 'epiphanies': brief sketches describing moments of unique revelations or rare insights into people and things. He also began to make notes for a novel which he was to call *Stephen Hero*. In his Dublin Diary Stanislaus claims to have given Joyce the title and in an entry under the date 29 March 1904, he tells us that eleven chapters had already been written. Stephen Hero grew very long indeed and was abandoned eventually or, more accurately perhaps, it was reconceived and subsumed in part as material for *A Portrait of the Artist as a Young Man*. There is a story that Joyce threw the manuscript of *Stephen Hero* on the fire but that Nora rescued it. Whether that is so or not, it was published eventually in an incomplete state some years after Joyce's death, although Joyce himself had dismissed it as a 'schoolboy production'.

According to Herbert Gorman, Joyce's first biographer, *Stephen Hero* was to be autobiographical, the story of the growth of his own mind, the story of Joyce's (I quote) 'own intensive absorption in himself, and what he had been, and how he had grown out of the Jesuitical garden of his youth. He endeavoured to see himself objectively, to assume a godlike pose of watchfulness over the small boy and youth he called Stephen and who was really himself.'

That godlike pose can become a bit trying for the reader of the published work and the aesthetic theory on which the Hero is working is set out so often and at such length that it can become wearisome. Nevertheless, *Stephen Hero* is important. It adds considerably to our understanding of

A Portrait of the Artist as a Young Man. We meet more of the characters who moved in and out of those adolescent experiences
and we are told more about how they looked and what they
said, which is particularly welcome in the case of those who
survived the subsequent literary metamorphosis. There is
much more background detail as well, about the house the
Joyces lived in, the individual members of the family, the
companions he walked with on those peripatetic wanderings.
It tells us more also about the squalor and deprivation and
drunkenness into which the life of the Joyce family was
declining in those formative years. The style veers from
youthful and self-conscious over-emphasis to passages that are
accomplished and controlled. For example:

> The mist of evening had begun to thicken into slow, fine
> rain and Stephen halted at the end of a narrow path beside
> a few laurel bushes, watching at the end of a leaf a tiny
> point of rain form and twinkle and hesitate and finally take
> the plunge into the sodden clay beneath. He wondered was
> it raining in Westmeath, were the cattle standing together
> patiently in the shelter of the hedges and reeking in the rain.

Nothing particularly godlike there, only the qualities of
economy and mood and observation. There are runs of
dialogue as accomplished as anything in *Portrait of the Artist*,
such as this exchange about the ceremonies of Holy Week:

> Isn't it strange to see the Mass of the Presanctified,
> said Stephen, no lights or vestments, the alter naked, the
> door of the tabernacle gaping open, the priests lying
> prostrate on the altar steps?
> Yes, said Cranley.
> Don't you think the Reader who begins the Mass is
> a strange person. No-one knows where he came from:
> he has no connection with the Mass. He comes out by
> himself and opens a book at the right hand side of the
> altar and when he has read the lesson he closes the book
> and goes away as he came. Isn't he strange?

Yes, said Cranley.

You know how his lesson begins? Haec Dicit dominus: in tribulatione sua mane consurgent ad me: venite et revertamur ad dominum – He chanted the opening of the lesson in mezza voce and his voice went flowing down the staircase and round the circular hall, each tone coming back upon the ear enriched and softened.

He pleads, said Stephen. He is what that chalk-faced chap was for me, advocatus diaboli. Jesus has no friend on Good Friday. –

I have referred to the squalor of those years. It was attributable entirely to the conduct of Joyce's father, who began marriage with a comfortable inheritance behind him and a sinecure of a job, but who squandered the one and lost the other through almost perpetual bouts of drinking. A little of this gets into both *Stephen Hero* and *A Portrait of the Artist*, but not as much as one would expect, given the circumstances of the case: a father out drinking while a young family waited at home with little, or often enough, no money at all for food. There is one description in *A Portrait of the Artist* of the family at tea:

> He pushed open the latchless door of the porch and passed through the naked hallway into the kitchen. A group of his brothers and sisters was sitting round the table. Tea was nearly over and only the last of the second watered tea remained in the bottoms of the small glass jars and jamjars which did service for tea cups. Discarded crusts and lumps of sugared bread, turned brown by the tea which had been poured over them, lay scattered on the table. Little wells of tea lay here and there on the board, and a knife with a broken ivory handle was stuck through the pith of a ravaged turnover.

Joyce was fond enough of his father to be extraordinarily tolerant of his shortcomings and content to list his attributes with a shrug of dismissal, describing him in *Portrait* as 'a medical student, an oarsman, a tenor, an amateur actor, a shouting politician, a small landlord, a small investor, a drinker, a good fellow, a story-teller, somebody's secretary, something in a distillery, a tax gatherer, a bankrupt and at present a praiser of his own past.'

Stanislaus had no such indulgence. He describes the gipsy-like flitting from house to house, nine different addresses in eleven years, because the father never paid rent. He records in his Dublin Diary under 26 July 1904:

> We have had very little food – no meal at all, in fact – and having taken some tea and dry bread, I washed and went out. Pappie came in sober, without money and in ill-humour, just as I was coming down the stairs. . . . We are this way through him having spent £2.10.0 on himself in the last 10 days.

Again, on 31 July 1904:

> I have been stripped of my garments, even my boots, to pawn them and feed on them. In what manner would we stand sickness?

In December 1904 he reports having lived for almost a year on starvation rations: a small breakfast, no dinner and no tea. He goes on later to make a list:

> I attribute the following to Pappie:
> (1) the undermining of his children's health, and their rotting teeth to absolutely irregular feeding and living, cheap adulterated food, and general unsanitary condi-tions of life
> (2) the handicap of his children's chances in life
> (3) Mother's unhealth, unhappiness, weakening mind and death on his moral brutality and the Juggernaut he made life with him and to his execrable treatment of her even up to her last day and
> (4) indirectly, Georgie's death, for if Georgie had been properly doctored or in hospital, he would have lived. Besides these he is pulling down his children's character with him as he sinks lower.

Perhaps that explains why in *Stephen Hero* Joyce, or more properly, the Hero, revels excessively in artistic theory and makes the mistake of thinking you theorise and then you write, whereas the fledged artist knows you write first and then rationalise – or let someone else do the rationalising for you. It is easy to believe there was a haunting need for some aesthetic of art and beauty as an armour against the vulgarity and squalor of the daily experience, the necessity for the escape of a spirit which fainted for want of order and beauty from a body that more often than not was in danger of fainting for want of bread.

In 1904 AE, who had read portions of *Stephen Hero*, asked Joyce for a short story which he later published in the *Irish Homestead* in July. The story was 'The Sisters', and it marked the beginning of his collection of short stories, *Dubliners*. The astonishing thing is that there is no trace in them of the distain or the weakness for high sentence which brand so much of *Stephen Hero* as adolescent. *Dubliners* as a collection is the work of an adult writer, a work described by L.A.G. Strong as a triumph of naturalism: quiet, accurate recordings of observed characters and conversations. If, in *Stephen Hero*, Joyce was exploring his own artistic intuitions and formulating his revolt against provincialism (as he saw it) and a national romanticism which he held to be false, in *Dubliners* he concentrated his cool and by no means humourless attention on the streets and the houses of Dublin. What he saw there reflected little of the refinements and highmindedness of accepted art. This parade of a society of spoiled priests, avaricious mothers, pimps, perverts, gamblers, drunkards and their exploited and acquiescent victims, sticks firmly to the unheroic view of the human condition, the banality of most of its blather, the dismissable nature of a large part of its preoccupations. He drew on the experiences of others as well as on his own encounters with everyday reality and did so without either rancour or sentiment. Where there is cruelty in what he has to say, it is not his, but that of the observed situation. And where there are victims there is understanding without sentimentality.

Dubliners was completed in 1905. After much argumentative correspondence and much dogged defence by Joyce of his methods and his material, it was published at last in the form he was determined on in 1914. A collection of his poems, *Chamber Music,* had been published in 1907.

Meanwhile, *Stephen Hero* had grown enormous but had got nowhere. Sylvia Beach says that when the manuscript was rejected by twenty publishers Joyce threw it on the fire. However that may be, he certainly abandoned it as a work of immaturity and began to re-cast the material in a form that could reflect his acquisition of wider technical skills. In *A Portrait of the Artist as a Young Man* he centralises the action in the mind of Stephen and imposes a stricter economy in the use of character and incident. The hankering after poetic expression for its own sake was abandoned, though heightened prose, in the form of carefully wrought rhythms and the quite lavish use of verbal colour is freely employed when the emotions are in climax and the imagination on fire. In *Portrait*, Theodore Spencer comments, we are looking at the room through a keyhole instead of an open door, by which he means, I think, that what we can see is given more impact because of things we know are there but *can't* see. Physically, there is still the tireless perambulating and the unflagging verbal explorations of literary Dublin, but technically he is now able to move with ease from the uncompromising and, where necessary, brutal presentation of exterior reality to the introspective and sensitive response, a wedding of what he had achieved in *Dubliners* with what he had attempted but failed to master in *Stephen Hero.* The enemies, however, remain the old ones, to be defeated or to be escaped from, as he makes clear throughout, and nowhere more so than in this oft-quoted passage:

> Stephen, following his own thought, was silent for an instant. The soul is born, he said vaguely, first in those moments I told you of. It has a slow and dark birth, more mysterious than the birth of the body. When the soul of a man is born in this country there are nets flung at it

to hold it back from flight. You talk to me of nationality, language, religion. I shall try to fly by those nets.

And later, he makes up his mind about what has to be done:

Look here, Cranley, he said, you have asked me what I would do and what I would not do. I will tell you what I will do and what I will not do. I will not serve that in which I no longer believe, whether it call itself my home, my fatherland or my church: and I will try to express myself in some mode of life or art as freely as I can and as wholly as I can, using for my defence the only arms I allow myself to use – silence, exile and cunning

On 8 October 1904 Joyce left Dublin with Nora Barnacle. I doubt his cunning and he can hardly be said to have remained silent, but, with the exception of a few short business visits, he stuck rigidly to the exile part of it until his death in Zurich in 1941.

1982